From the S

Spiritual Reflections from the Everyday

From the Sanctuary:

Spiritual Reflections from the Everyday

Peter Madsen Gubi

First published 2023
by Revd Professor Peter M. Gubi
c/o The Book Room
Moravian Church House
5 Muswell Hill
London N10 3TJ

Printed and bound in the UK by
TJ Books Limited
Padstow PL28 8RW

Cover designed by the
LIS Graphics Team
University of Chester

A catalogue record for this book is available from the British Library

ISBN 978-1-399951-20-3

FSC
www.fsc.org
MIX
Paper from responsible sources
FSC® C013056

This book is dedicated to my father,
Revd Peter Madsen Gubi, M.A.,
and to all those fellow pilgrims whom I have met on
my journey, who have taught me so much

Contents

Introduction

Many of Jesus' parables contain spiritual wisdom found in the everyday. This book follows that tradition of reflecting on observations from the everyday to discern the spiritual wisdom that can be gained for living life. The reflections follow the pattern and seasons of the Gregorian calendar and the seasons of the Christian Church. Each reflection is informed by psychological and theological insights, and asks the reader to pause and consider the relevance of the wisdom to their own life. The reflections were written over a 12-year period which included the Covid-19 pandemic. The 'Sanctuary' is the name given to my study at the bottom of my garden, which I use for my academic and religious preparations, and counselling and pastoral supervision practice. Welcome to reflections 'From the Sanctuary'.

Please note that the views, reflections and observations expressed in this book are those of the author alone, and not those of the Moravian Church.

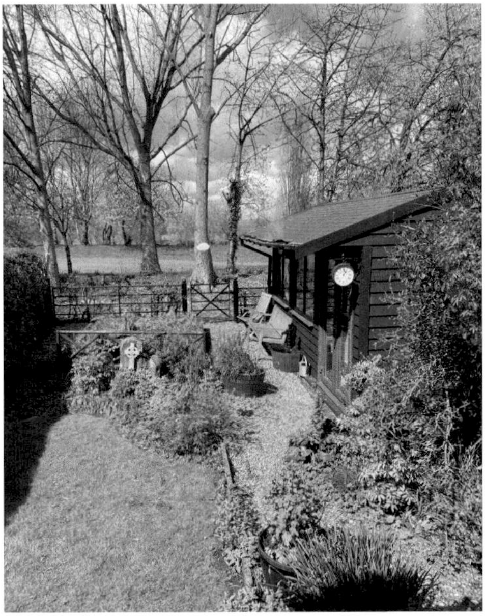

Crossing the threshold

Crossing the threshold of a New Year often brings with it an expectation of opportunity for change. There is a desire to create new resolutions; a wish for something to be different in various aspects of our lives. We annually cross this threshold in hope. Yet, the reality is that often little, if anything, changes. New resolutions are soon breached as we resort to familiar patterns of being and doing, in spite of our best intentions. Default positions kick in as we unconsciously act out well-practised attitudes and behaviours. Our hopes wither and deflate, and we chastise ourselves with 'whatever happened to our New Year resolutions'?

Perhaps, our mistake is in thinking that something fundamental can change simply because it is a New Year! The hope of a New Year message rarely emphasises the effort and discipline that is needed for fundamental change. It is given over to God and our good intention, with little investment of effort, to bring about the change. Yet, change within 'self', including spiritual growth (never mind dieting!), is more like a rock climb than a fell walk. Each 'hold' has to be gingerly sought out and tested, and invested with trust, before the full weight of a fundamental shift within our 'self' can occur. It requires building strength and fostering discipline. It is a 'working-at' process rather than an 'arrived-at' process.

If one studies scripture from many faith traditions, one finds that spiritual growth often occurs through wounds and setbacks, exile and wilderness. Resurrection seems not to be able to happen without crucifixion. To move on in faith is often to experience, endure, and then transcend, the scrapes and bruises that life presents – much as a rock climber has to feel and overcome the tiredness in arm and leg, and the pain of the scratching and knocking of limbs against hard, sharp rock. Yet, it is through experiencing, enduring, and then transcending the pain, that stronger glimpses of the light and the truth of God can be experienced as healing and growth-enhancing. Spiritual growth and change require discipline and effort: daily prayer; small acts of grace; little shifts in thinking such as gradually learning to see glimpses of Christ in all things and all people; reading scripture and applying its wisdom to personal circumstance; conversing with fellow pilgrims. These all add to the gentle ploughing of new furrows in spiritual well-being. Expectations of large leaps and strides, or the hasty ploughing of new furrows, are unrealistic. They lack the underpinning test of trust that acts as the foothold for the next small move needed to enact change.

So, this New Year, may we resolve to see the value and miracle of small, but nonetheless significant, shifts, as we work at the discipline that is required for fundamental change in our spiritual lives, and in other aspects of life. May we come to foster realistic expectation, and embrace the gingerly-made steps as being more fundamental than the large leap that carries fragile promise – but which is likely to be broken because it is fragile. For in doing that, we won't be disappointed when we cross the threshold of this New Year.

Let there be light

Last night, I couldn't sleep. 'Things' were playing on my mind, as 'things' can do at 3am. I found myself feeling low, and generally angry with God. All I was hearing on the radio in the small hours of the morning, was yet another bombing, and yet more threats from terrorism. "How many more peace candles, and prayers for peace, do we have to say before there is peace?!" I was saying to God in my angry prayers.

Just as I had got that off my chest (for prayer, I find, often changes my perspective on things), God answered! The depressing news on the radio was followed by an encouraging article on how many people, who are in prison because of drug addiction, have used their experience to re-educate themselves, and have made a success of their lives once they are on day release. Examples were given of a lady who learned floristry and on release, she had set up her own business using the skills and advice of The Prince's Trust. Now, a few years later, she had three outlets to her business and was employing others. She had gone from being unemployable because of her prison record, to being an employer. I also know of a friend who, once imprisoned, learned to read and write Braille, and spent his time translating books for the blind. Now, he has set up his own business and is using his skills in a new direction, giving him a sense of purpose again.

Out of the darkness has shone forth light! This is the message of Christmas, but not the message only for Christmas. It is one that we need reminding of, day by day, as we begin a New Year – that however bleak things may look from time to time, or whatever twists and turns our lives may take, God is in it with us. There is always light in the darkness if we can but see it; and if we can keep enough of that light (that awareness of God and of goodness) in our vision of life, we can maintain a sense of hope and optimism in a seemingly bleak world. Whether there is more darkness than light, or more light than darkness, depends largely on the attitude we bring to life; and our faith can help us see more of the light if we choose to remember it, and to live with an awareness of God constantly in our lives.

With more light than darkness in our vision – more of God than doom in what we see, and how we regard what is happening to us and our world – let us embrace the opportunities of a New Year with hope and gratitude. Let there be light!

What to do?

Last week, I went to meet a colleague at Chester train station. After parking my car in a side road, I had to walk past a young lady who was aged in her late teens or early twenties. She was sitting on the pavement. She was shivering; she had a tear-stained face; she was clearly homeless and she was begging for money. Not knowing what to do, I walked past her, inappropriately bidding her 'good morning'. At least in doing so, I had acknowledged her humanity (I kidded myself).

As I waited for my colleague's train to arrive, I was flooded with guilt for 'walking by on the other side'. In amongst the guilt, I recognised that I was feeling enormous care, compassion and concern for her – even though I had never met her before. I wondered what had brought her to that lowest point in her life? I wanted to rescue her – to take her home, to give her the opportunity for warmth, a shower, some food and a bed – and to try and help her sort her life out (as if I could!). I wanted to look after her, but I knew that in today's safeguarding society, acting from that place of compassion was inappropriate. The irony was not lost on me that in needing to protect myself, she remained at risk. I felt paralysed by not knowing how to help her – so like most of us, I did nothing.

I was distracted from this inner turmoil of thoughts and feelings by the arrival of my colleague. I said nothing to him about it, but I silently assuaged my guilt, on the way back to the car, by slipping her a £10 note. Her face lit up, full of appreciation. I hoped that that might go towards paying for a bed for the night – but I knew that it might probably go towards her next 'fix'. She could have been my daughter, my niece, or my god-daughter. Aargh ...! What to do?!

And, as Christians, we have Jesus' words in Matthew 25:40–45, that "*whatever we do for one of the least of these brothers and sisters, we do for him*". These words seem tough to live out at times – particularly when we are blessed, have plenty and much privilege. I can do what almost everyone else does, and that is to blame the politicians for the issue of homelessness – that way it isn't my problem; or I can turn away from the enormity of the problem in our cities and towns by simply doing nothing other than to hope that someone else will deal with the problem; or I can remind myself of words from James 2: 14–26, that "*faith without action is dead*", and do what I can do to help.

What might you do in such circumstances(?) – because the homeless are only just down the road in the doorways of our cities. It's tough being a Christian sometimes, especially when encountering the more shadowed realities of life.

Subtle guidance

Sometimes, it is amazing where spiritual guidance comes from, and how God speaks to us.

A recent journey through the picturesque Pennines, between Cumbria and West Yorkshire, found me lost – simply because I ignored the instructions that my satnav was giving me. I thought I knew better and so ignored its demands for me to turn around because I was convinced that I was going in the right direction; but rather than going south-east, I was in fact heading north-east. When Darlington began to show on the signs as I searched for Kirkby Lonsdale, I thought I'd better take notice! I didn't know best after all.

Whilst it was still light, I enjoyed the scenery with the delicate snow on the peaks contrasting with the ruggedness of the slopes of the Pennines; but because my journey took three hours longer than intended, night soon fell – and so did a thick, dense fog that only Yorkshire does so well. Now, having eaten humble pie and desperately trusting my satnav, I was led through some 'interesting' back roads and country lanes, over hill and down dale (having told it to avoid motorways because I do so much motorway travel and wanted a change). But, because of the fog, I couldn't see a thing as it was so thick, and often I couldn't even see the verges of the road, except that some were snow-lined. If it hadn't been for this, I'm sure I would have been ditch-bound somewhere on a moor. It was a bit scary at times.

Once I eventually emerged from the moors into the urban terrain of Keighley, feeling somewhat tired and stressed from having to concentrate in the fog for so long, I was forced to stop at a red traffic light outside a carpet shop. On looking to my left through the passenger window, there, hanging in the shop window, was a large blue rug with the emboldened words – "Keep calm and carry on!" It was just what I needed to 'hear' to see me through the rest of my journey, which was nearing its end.

This escapade led me to reflect on how, in faith, we have the tools, the wisdom from the ages through Scripture, and the values to live a good life and fulfil our potential – as God intends for us. Yet, we have within us a stubbornness to do it our way. Some call it 'free will' – others might justifiably call it 'stupidity'. Yet, even when we go wrong, God continually guides, if only we can see it and notice the signs. It may be in obvious ways, like the satnav – but also in less obvious ways like the snow on the verges, or a passing word (like the rug), which keep us going in the best way. May we be open to God's word and direction in our lives. May we see and hear His subtle and not so subtle word for us, so that we can become the best that He intends.

Epiphany

Whatever the literal truth of the Birth Narratives of Jesus, they ooze spiritual truth! After the trauma of Advent, characterised by patient journeying, expectation and anticipation, comes 'epiphany': that realisation that God is among us, and is available for relationship to all people (symbolised in the Birth Narratives as the visit of the Wise Men who were rich, powerful, wise and Gentile). They stand in stark comparison to the Shepherds who symbolise the poor, uneducated and Jewish). And that truth of the possibility of relationship with God, and encounter with the sacred, still exists – for all people; not just for religious or holy people, or even just Christian believers. It is the realisation that God is in everything and every situation – even in the secular and profane – if only we can see it. Epiphany can mean a sudden, intuitive perception of, or insight into, the reality or essential meaning of something, usually initiated by some simple, homely, or commonplace occurrence or experience – such as the realisation that God is in all things, and in all encounters, if we can have the openness to that possibility within our outlook on life. That idea of God being in all things may be particularly challenging at the moment, just when we have had our hopes dashed, and our expectations disappointed because of the resurgence of the pandemic. However, God is there if we can see Him.

One small example of that is that, in the summer, I lost my cat, 'Effie', after she became too poorly to continue living. I had had her for 18 years, and there was a real sense of sadness at the loss of her, and of there being a void in our household as a result of her passing. We debated about whether to replace her, and my father's wise words at the time were, "wait a bit and see what happens". What happened after 'a bit' was that a little stray cat, whom we have now called 'Marusha' has adopted us. She carries the name of another cat that was similarly coloured, which we had in Barbados. She has been a real blessing to us, and an epiphany in our lives, as God has encountered us through her. And she is only one of many examples of our lives being blessed during this time of disappointment – of light in the darkness.

away the fear of snow and enable its exciting and transformational quality to endure – it needs to be worked through over time in order to release us into a new and transformed way of looking at the world and at our 'self'.

So, I wish for you a transformational year ahead – one that becomes gradually filled with an awareness of God's love and a closely-felt sense of God's loving presence in your life, as you journey forth. What a gift to yourself that would be!

Where is God?

How do we cope (or not), when things don't go *our* way? This is very much in my mind as I deal with the frustration of not being able to be punctual for an event, and I am delayed in the visiting that I had hoped to do today. For I write this, not in my Sanctuary, but in the local Honda garage, as I await the fixing of my car in response to a warning light that came on as I journeyed to my meeting. The warning light indicates that the problem is serious and needs to be fixed urgently, and I am aware that the car is unusually sluggish in its response to the accelerator. So, my well-laid plans are thwarted! Aarrggh! Once I get past the initial frustration of having my intentions thwarted, and the guilt of having let others down, I am trying to see where God may be in all of this.

Some people hold the view that everything that happens is God's Will. God intended it to happen, or it would not have happened – or 'nothing can happen unless God wills it'. Whilst I think that that philosophical approach does hold some validity (with *huge* reservations), I am confronted with the difficulty that that view is of no comfort to those who are in the immediacy of their struggle and suffering. There is no comfort at all in the argument that suffering abuse, conflict, torture – let alone in thinking the insignificant struggles with my car – are God's Will.

However, I do find it helpful to ask 'where is God *in* this?' God can be present, and experienced, in the midst of any suffering and evil. "*Where could I go to escape from you? Where could I get away from your presence? If I went up to heaven, you would be there; if I lay down in Sheol (Hell), you would be there ...*" (Psalm 139:7–8). My minor frustrations with my car, give me an important lesson that life is not in my control. And actually, the experience (whether it be God's Will or not) has enabled encounters with others at the Honda garage that I would not have otherwise experienced. It has also enabled these thoughts to emerge and be written. So, God can be present, and alongside us, in all our struggles and our frustrations, if we can but see His presence.

So, I invite you to take some time out to recall the frustrations and struggles in your life, and ask yourself, 'Where is God in them?' Discerning the presence of God in all things can help to make some sense of our experiences.

Feeling stagnant

Though it may feel as if everything has gone stagnant, know that this is the season in which God is gathering together more resources to continue his masterpiece.

My sense of 'stagnancy' may have something to do with being surrounded by winter, when, in nature, little happens. This seems to mirror my life at this time of year. It is easy for me to think of a time of seeming 'stagnancy' – when nothing new or growthful seems to be happening – as a time when nothing is actually occurring; and yet the expectation of 'continual shifting' and growth is something that has only recently become a 'cultural norm' in our history, as part of the capitalist mantra that surrounds us. We see it in economic life, when perpetual 'growth' in profits is emphasised. This makes it seem that there is something 'wrong' with an organisation if growth does not continue, year-on-year; and something wrong in our lives if we are not embracing some new venture, year-on-year; or increasing our productivity. However, that is unrealistic. Just as there is a 'finiteness' to growth, there *must* be times of consolidation and taking-stock – when nothing outwardly seems to be happening – even in our spiritual life. Yet, as in a stagnant pool, life *is* happening. Organisms are thriving. Some organisms may die from the seeming lack of movement; but others grow. Relating it back to our spiritual life, so called 'times of stagnancy' can be a time of sifting, discernment and reflection – when we need to be still, and embrace the mundane, in order to listen to the still small voice of God, and to find the fingerprints of God in the day-to-day.

As winter is outwardly a time of standing still – when nature bunkers down – what is actually happening is a time of rejuvenation and rest; a necessary time of readiness for the right moment when the temperature (or climate) allows more outward signs of movement and growth. Being in that place of seeming stagnancy is to trust that this is the season in which God is gathering together more resources to continue his masterpiece. Nothing is wasted in our spiritual lives – even our spiritual winters.

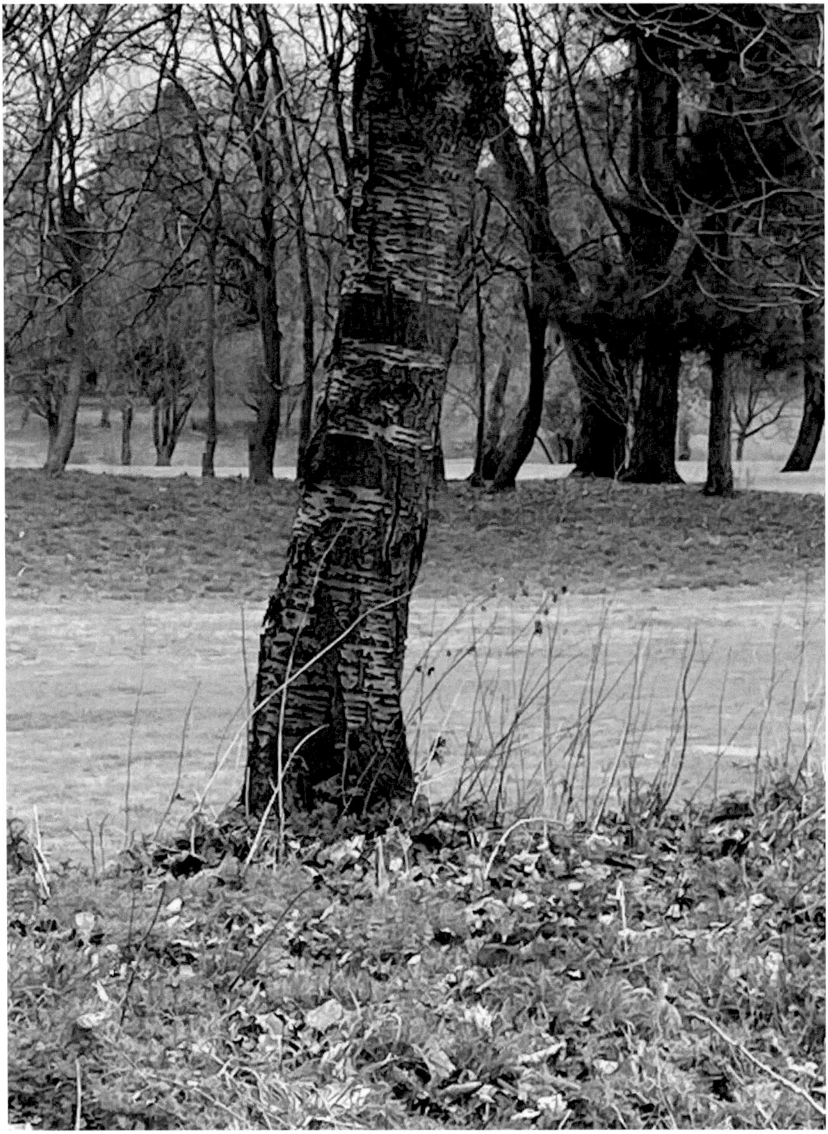

Surviving spiritual attack

A few months ago, I went away for a weekend. On my return, I discovered that my neighbour had torn up part of the hedge between her property and mine, and had installed a wooden fence to border a newly-created patio on her side.

Although it didn't come as a complete surprise (for she had asked me how I would feel if she did it – but hadn't indicated when it would be done), I was left with some temporary feelings of bereavement. The small hedge sparrows fly in and out of that hedge. What would happen to them? I miss seeing them in that part of the hedge, although much of the hedge, further down the garden, remains. I prefer natural barriers, like hedges (although I hate cutting them). Wooden fences seem largely 'characterless' to me, although I understand the practicality of them. Had she made that part of my garden into something featureless?

After my initial loss, my attention then turned to concern about my electricity supply to the Sanctuary. It comes from the main house, and is channelled through reinforced cable which runs on the surface of the garden *at the base of the hedge* (so that I know its location when I'm digging to avoid electrocuting myself when gardening). 'Had the cabling been spared in so rapid a fence construction', I wondered. Fortunately, to my relief, it had survived intact.

Two spiritual reflections came from this event for me: the first is that, in my experience, it feels as though life sometimes conspires against the things that we hold to be precious. It feels particularly so to me, sometimes, in relation to faith. There are so many 'rational' arguments and scientific reasons why faith is questionable, and so many people saying it is 'stupid' to believe ("I can't believe that someone as intelligent as you can still believe that rubbish!"); but faith is not from a rational or scientific domain. It reflects a mystical, spiritual and largely inexpressible dimension to life. It is a dimension that we can experience, but cannot always put into words; and when we try to explain, it is immediately limited by language – yet it is precious, because it is deeply meaningful.

Leviticus shows that God is concerned with the detail of our lives, and that our lives would be lived better if we were concerned more about God in the detail of everything that we do.

Whilst God has been taken out of much in society, many of the political messages we are surrounded by regarding climate change and single-use plastic (to name but only two) have, at their core, the necessity for good stewardship of our planet – a biblical principle found in Leviticus. Therefore, God *is* in it. Much of the antidote to the hate in society is found in Leviticus – "*Love your neighbour as you love yourself*" (19:17–18) – a principle that is found at the centre of the work of many charities and individuals, but without acknowledgement of God; yet their work is of God. It is all ancient wisdom from ancient Israel, which, if strayed too far away from, results in struggle, conflict and destruction – for us and for society. Guidance for our well-being and wholeness rests within living close to what God wills – yet this ancient wisdom is often so easily cast aside. So – how can you live in such a way that has God, and holiness, more at the centre of your life? For in that, lies our well-being, wholeness and salvation – as individuals and as society.

Trust the process

'Trust the process' is a mantra that I say to myself, as a Counsellor, at those times when I am working with a client and I am not sure where s/he is, or is going, in their psychological journey; or I realise that I am pushing the client beyond where they are psychologically 'ready' to go, or I am wanting some direction for him/her more than s/he is wanting it for their self. 'Trusting the process' is a means of holding on to hope for the client, and of trusting in their capacity for change and growth – at their pace, rather than at mine, and in the direction that is right for them rather than the one that I think is right for them. If I can just 'trust the process', then the change, direction and growth will be revealed in the fullness of time. For me, it is akin to saying, 'trust God'. God's Will will be revealed – in time. I just have to be patient and to trust. It is so easy to say, yet sometimes so hard to live – especially when we are needing certainty and direction, trying to be helpful (on our terms), and we are not at ease with feeling helpless or vulnerable.

I recently took on a new client who, in the first session, said that he didn't do 'reflective' (i.e. he didn't 'do' standing back from his feelings and trying to make some sense of where they had come from and, with that knowledge, think about how he might respond differently in certain situations). If I were to imagine and describe him as an object, I would say that I experienced him in the first session as a 'locked padlock'. After the session, I found myself searching for 'the key' to enable me to help him, whereas after further reflection, what I discovered was that I needed to trust in my capacity as a metaphorical 'locksmith'. With my need to 'do' and to 'break in' abated, I simply sat alongside him in the second session and, lo and behold, that next session was very different. With some trust having been built up in the relationship, he soon opened up to some areas of vulnerability with which we were able to work sensitively. He had 'unlocked'. From how I had experienced him in the first session, I was left with awe and wonder at his ability to be 'reflective', having said that it wasn't 'his thing'.

The scriptures contain many narratives of people who have sat with helplessness but who have trusted God and, in time, the will of God has been revealed. Not necessarily in the time required by those who wish He would act sooner – but in God's time ... And what has emerged has been even more wonderful than they could have imagined. So, can we trust the process? Can we trust God? If so, we can reach a place of acceptance more easily, and let go of our disappointment, and just 'be' with what is, rather than carry the frustration of what we feel 'should' be. 'Trust the process' – because God is in it.

Be wary of strategising

I was noticing the other day, just how blessed I was feeling to have my 'Sanctuary'. It is sometimes called 'your shed' or 'your man cave' by others, but when it is, I notice that I become defensive. It is definitely my 'Sanctuary'. It is the place where I feel inspired and reflective; where I prepare my services from; where I write my academic papers and books. It is where I feel in prayer, and where I feel close to God. These days, it has also become my day-to-day place of work, but that hasn't detracted from the felt sense of specialness – or 'set-aside-ness'.

Yet, it wasn't a planned build. It was built in response to the death of my mother. It emerged out of a place of grief, which manifested itself in a desire to protect my dad – to hold on to him so that I wouldn't lose them both. I knew that if he was to come and live with me (because he had had a number of falls and lived some distance away), I would have to move my 'study' out of the spare bedroom, so that it could become his room. The natural solution to the situation was to build a space in the garden. What I couldn't have foreseen, was just how valuable a space it would be to work from in a pandemic!

We seem to be culturally-imbued with a mindset that says that building strategy and planning is necessary for advancement. Even in the Church, we are continually invited to consider our strategy for mission and evangelism – and whilst that makes us feel that we are doing something, we forget that, ultimately, it is God who determines.

Joseph could never have known that he would become the second person in Egypt when his brothers sold him into slavery. Ruth could never have known how inspiring her story would be, particularly to women. Neither of them could have planned or strategised their way into the Old Testament. Instead, they simply followed their faith journey, and God 'used' them in His work. Now they are examples to us as their situations 'speak' into our own with wisdom and spiritual insight.

Whilst having a strategy may refresh our vision and focus our thinking, let us never lose sight of where God is already at work in our lives, and in our Church community. For God is already among us. Any man-made strategy or directionality needs to be held lightly, for as Proverbs 16:9 says: "*A man's heart plans his way, but the* L*ORD directs his steps.*"

By another road

In Matthew 2:12, it says, "*Then they returned to their country by another road, since God had warned them in a dream not to go back to Herod.*"

"*Then they returned to their country by another road …*" During the last 18 months, I have felt lucky not to have to travel to work in Chester as much, because almost all of my work can be done 'From the Sanctuary' via my computer and internet. However, the times that I have had to go into Chester, have meant having to find 'another road' as the A51 has been completely closed in one part, where the road has been gradually slipping into the canal, near Barbridge. I guess that Highways England took advantage of the quieter traffic flow, in order to carry out the major roadworks – which certainly needed doing. At first, I found this disruption to my usual routine to be a nuisance, as I had to leave home earlier and find a different way; but then I began to embrace it as an opportunity (and a challenge) to find new routes to work – each taking me through parts of Cheshire that I had never ventured to before. Many of my new routes took me through really beautiful countryside and villages which I may go back to and look around on my bike (when/if I get any time to do so), as some of it has been through gorgeous country roads, with some stunning scenery and village architecture.

I wonder if the Magi felt inconvenienced by having to return to their country by another road, as we often do when the journey of life doesn't happen as we have planned it. Yet, as for them, often, God is in it. We can see God's presence (and possibly purpose) if we are able to stand back from our annoyance and frustration, and sink into a new sense of wonder and opportunity to do things differently, and see or experience new things that we have never had the opportunity to encounter before.

What things in life are not happening in the usual way you think they should? Can you step back from your disappointment and frustration, and see God in what is being enabled? For if, and when, you do, peace and delight can often replace the angst. God *is* in it.

Snowdrops of Lent

My most favourite plants in the garden are snowdrops. I have spent years stocking the garden with them when I can find them. They are particularly difficult to buy. No one seems to stock them; but over the years, I have found them here and there to buy – not to dig up from the verges (although I have been tempted)! Sometimes, students and friends have given me some. I have also found a garden centre nearby that occasionally stocks them, but they soon sell out and are popular with others too. So, it is a matter of keeping looking, and of being there when they have them. A place I love to visit at this time of year is Rode Hall, on the Staffordshire/Cheshire border, which has snowdrop walks through masses and masses of snowdrops which are growing wild. This year, my snowdrops have looked especially magnificent in the garden, so much so that I haven't needed my Rode Hall fix. They have spread and filled the garden in the way that I had eventually hoped they would. My anticipation and vision have been fulfilled, and I can now really enjoy them and feel a deep gratitude while among them.

Lent is supposed to be a time in the Christian calendar which is characterised as a period of spiritual anticipation, discernment and preparation. In a way, it is a time of metaphorically planting spiritual snowdrops in readiness for the growth and spiritual fruition of what we plant. Lent is a time of reflection – a time of prayer and study, and of asking what God wants from us. How can I bring my life more in touch with the aliveness of God's Holy Spirit, and grow in such a way to reflect more of the Glory and Grace of God? How can I adjust my life so that I can sit more with the love and blessing of God's comforting presence? It is difficult to achieve with a working life and a hectic family life – but stopping for a while to just be among the snowdrops, with a spirit of gratitude and sense of blessedness, is one way of being more with God. May you find your snowdrop moments throughout Lent.

the troubled and vulnerable around us? It really doesn't matter what I (or you) want, like or don't like. What is important here, is God.

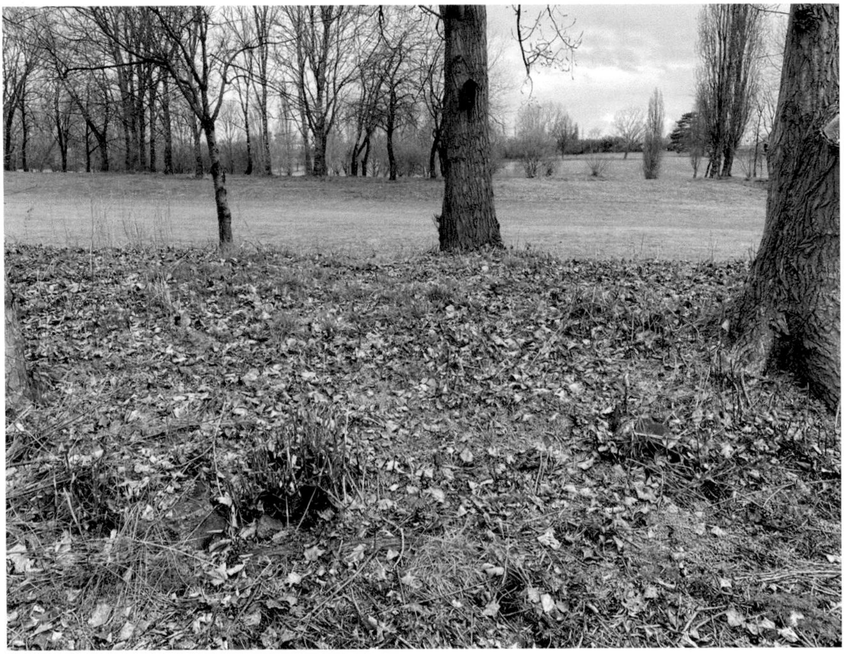

The limitation of language

As I am sat here in my Sanctuary, observing the squirrels running amongst the snowdrops and dwarf cyclamens, I am left reflecting on how limited language is in capturing what I am feeling. My feelings include awe, wonder, gratitude, privilege, blessing ... the list could go on – and yet none of those words quite capture the experience.

My pause for reflection comes from just having read through a draft of a student's chapter for her doctoral thesis, in which she is seeking to research 'moments of love' in the therapeutic relationship. I know from a personal, felt sense of experiencing what she is trying to capture, but it is clear that none of her definitions of 'love' quite encapsulate what she is trying to research. How do you define 'love'? What words can adequately capture it for all occasions – let alone for the purposes of research?

I am often similarly interested when people say that they don't believe in 'God', but yet they can often acknowledge a sense of the spiritual (transcendence; life-giving and creative energy; connection with something bigger than ourselves). What is it precisely that they don't believe in then, because those words speak to me of 'God'? Similarly, when people have a faith in God, what is it precisely in which they have a faith? What does the term 'believe in' mean exactly? My experience is that when people of faith and no faith put these issues under the microscope in mutual conversation, and struggle with definitions, they actually end up having more in common than they have that is different. So, is the limitation of language that which prohibits a belief in God?

In Church, we often think that we have a shared experience of the presence of God, because we all claim to share a Christian faith – but do we have a shared experience? How 'common' is common worship? Is faith more personal than shared, I wonder?

These complexities and limitations of language mean that arguing faith matters in a rational, intellectual way can never be done satisfactorily. You can't win people over to God through an argument – although many theologians have tried. Like observing the squirrels,

(Re)creation

For me, spring is a time of (re)creation, bringing forth frolicking lambs, beautiful spring flowers and increasing day length. Easter, also, will soon be upon us, with its spiritual emphasis on (re)creation – life out of death; resurrection out of crucifixion; new out of old. It is a time of hope, in which we can develop our ability to see 'that it is good' (i.e. all life is 'of God'; it contains His fingerprints, and it has a sacredness).

My reflections were recently focused on the first of the creation narratives at the beginning of Genesis (1:1–31) – in which God 'brings forth' (i.e. creates), and sees that what He has created is 'very good'. It is a familiar narrative to me, with a repetitive 'poetic' pattern to the description of the creation of each day ("*In the beginning ... And God said, 'Let there be ...', Evening came and morning came, the ... day.*") Yet, what particularly resonated with me this time, was in seeing (for the first time) the seventh day as being an equally important part of God's creation. Previously, I had only seen creation as the description of what was happening on the first six days, with the seventh day being a day of rest (i.e. a time of non-creation).

Yet, rest is a *crucial* part of (re)creation. By sometimes stopping, and 'putting down', and relaxing, we are being (re)created. Recovery, recuperation and relaxation are necessary aspects of God (re)creating us – hence in our 'recreation', we do things that benefit us mentally, physically and spiritually (e.g. walking, gardening, watching films, reading books, playing with Lego, etc.), and in which we find fun.

For someone like me, who has a strong work ethic, having rest – let alone having fun – is a constant challenge. There is always something 'to do' or something that is waiting 'to be done'; someone in need, or someone who is waiting to be visited. Yet, recognising the importance of recreation in God's intention for us as human beings – who need to be (re)created – is crucial to our spiritual, our mental and our physical well-being. To be out of balance in each of these three areas of our lives, is not to live as God intended us to be. Our body carries this tacit wisdom, if only we can learn to listen to it. We listen and respond when it is hungry, or has a sexual urge, or is enduring a headache. Why do the world, there is still hope. So, we bring out the chocolate eggs and rabbits, and the little yellow fluffy chickens that the commercial world provides – all symbols of the new life which is to be celebrated and marvelled at – but actually, and more profoundly, which is already in the emerging world that is present around us.

Take a gentle stroll and enjoy the sight and symbolism that is Easter – but remember what happened to Christ as you journey, and be filled with hope. Moravians haven't been called 'the Easter People' for nothing!

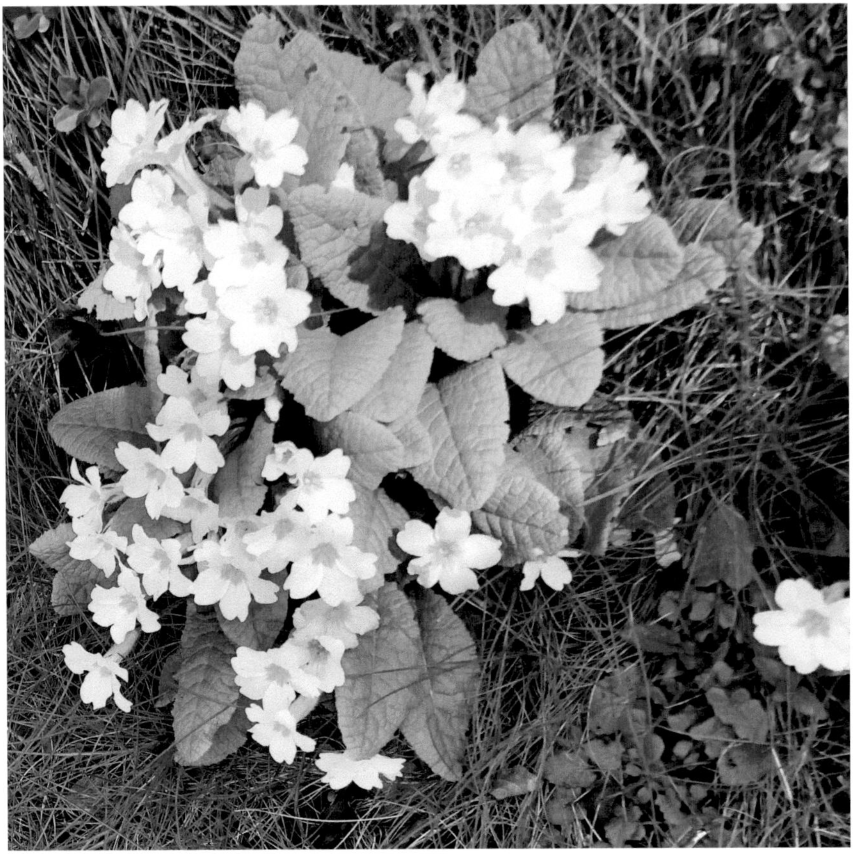

Hope for the 'now'

Last summer, I was enjoying a walk by the River Dove in Derbyshire, when I came across a tree that had fallen. Under the circumstances, it should have died. Yet it was resilient enough to grow again when everything was stacked against it. Something inside was enabling it to have a second chance, so much so, that it was growing from two places on the fallen trunk, and will eventually become two trees!

In my counselling work, I have met many people like that tree. Tragedy or trauma has affected their life. Their familiar world has fallen through, and they have been plummeted into the freefall of uncertainty and vulnerability. Yet, after a period of counselling and support, something inside of them has been reawakened (the Divine spark, perhaps), and has enabled them to find the resources to embrace life again – sometimes enabling them to live a 'richer' life; not necessarily in a more material way, but in a way that encompasses better values or a sense of greater purpose than before. Tragedy can often show us what is important in life.

I see these experiences as 'crucifixion' and 'resurrection' – when from death, new life comes. Often (but sadly, not always) the quality of life that emerges from the death of the old familiar life, is better. It's as if the rubble of the old life is used to build a new set of foundations for the new life. It is inspiring to witness, and offers hope to others who are in freefall, and hope to those of us who accompany those in life's freefall. I often find that witnessing it when it happens strengthens my faith, and I can see the importance of the resurrection event to our Christian faith. People often think that resurrection is a sign of hope for the life hereafter; but to me, resurrection offers hope for life now.

it becomes meaningful only when one's heart is open to the presence of awe and wonder of God – and to the presence and spirit of the living Lord. It is a tacit knowing, formed through a heart relationship, rather than through 'understanding'. To rationalise and intellectualise the experiencing of the observation of the squirrels, takes something of fundamental importance away from what one is trying to capture and communicate. Likewise, to speak of God and faith in a rational, intellectual way, in order to try and convince others of its truth, will seldom succeed. Indeed, we may actually achieve the opposite, and drive them away.

Yet, the truth of God is still undeniably present. I can still experience and know the reality of the presence of squirrels, and the presence of God, in my life – more than just what I can see. I know them through a felt-response to what I am experiencing of them both. Similarly, I can still experience and know the reality of another's love, and my love for another. Their existence is not what is in doubt. Our struggle, then, is in enabling others to experience God for themselves. Only then will their eyes and hearts be truly opened. Christ said, "*if they have ears, then let them hear*" (Matthew 11:15) – but I wonder if what He actually meant was, 'if they want to know me, let their hearts encounter me'.

New life

What a wonderful time of year this is! Spring is with us! In my garden, spring started to demand my attention with the clumps of snowdrops ..., then the cyclamens and crocuses popped up in clusters to join them ..., and now the daffodils are beginning to show their majestic golden yellow heads and dark green, spear-like leaves – dancing in the breeze. What a beautiful sight! New life! Lambs are frolicking in the pastures. Soon there will be bluebells. In the earlier hours of the daybreak, rabbits hop around on the hillsides nibbling the grass, and birdsong greets the break of the morn – an amazing sound to behold. There are leaves on some of the trees, and the rest are in bud. There is a resurrection taking place around us as nature safely emerges from the battening down of winter. Gone, hopefully, is the harshness of winter, although some snow is still possible, as nature is caressed by the life-enabling shafts of warm sunlight. Yet it is still risky for new life, as night frost has the potential to end it with its icy sword. It isn't yet a time to plant out seedlings, except under cover.

Easter is the time when we celebrate this transition from 'death' to new life, which is inherent in nature and in our faith, by celebrating the resurrection of Christ. The winter of humanity that brought an end to a good and gracious life was recalled during the nightly readings of the 'Harmony of the Gospel' during 'Passion Week' (i.e. the week before Easter). It is a moving narrative that culminates in the events of Good Friday, which is a day of remembering when Christ was crucified – when we see the worst of humanity (that of which we are all capable) in action. Yet, even in that, we see God's presence in the grace of Christ as he faces his oppressors with humility and vulnerability. Then, three days later, we had the re-emergence of hope from despair, seen in the risen Christ on Easter Day. We take this to be a spiritual truth that there is life beyond death, and so we celebrate this with an early morning service. In many Moravian Churches, this takes place in God's Acre (our burial ground) on Easter Day – remembering those who have passed on to better things, but who have left an imprint on our lives, our souls and our community. It reminds us that even if we face the worst of

Transcending our wants

In my profession, there is an approach to psychotherapy known as 'psychosynthesis'. It embraces 'the spiritual' and encompasses a particular 'technique' (which I find useful) in which, after issues have been talked through and 'felt' at various levels, finally 'higher wisdom' is sought and is invited to 'speak' into the situation. The therapist may gently invite the client to choose a stone (or an object from a range of objects) that represents the wiser part of their 'self'. After spending a few moments getting in touch with that part of 'self' and listening carefully to it (putting aside ego and injury), the client is invited to transcend their immediate difficulties and speak from that part of their 'wiser self' into the situation. It can be very powerful and cathartic to do as a client, and to witness happening as a therapist.

Sometimes, we get bogged down in our grievances and disappointments, and we struggle to get past our sense of injury. It manifests itself when we hear ourselves say something like: "It wasn't what I would have done!" or "I don't like that/it" or "I wasn't consulted, so I won't play ball." We are all guilty of that at times. Entwined in that is some sense that 'I', and what 'I want' and 'like', are what the decision of the Church should have been about – rather than it being about God.

Although we are all important, it is wiser at times not to make too much of our own importance. In the context of the Church, I gain some sense of smallness and humility when I think of the bigger history and journey of our Church – and of all those journeys made before mine by the great cloud of witnesses by whom we are encompassed (Hebrews 12:1). When considered with that lens, my opinions, likes and dislikes are utterly insignificant and truly unimportant. What does it matter what I (or you) like or don't like? What is important is in discerning what God would say or want to happen.

As God *is* with us, what is S/He saying? Where is the voice of that greater spiritual wisdom, speaking into our situation? How does what we decide to do: further His/Her work, reflect His/Her values; help us to spread the Good News (Gospel); or better enable us to show love to

May every day be an epiphany as we encounter God in everyone we meet, and in every situation in which we find ourselves. It's a wonderful attitude to develop that will help us to transform each day, and gives a different perspective on our ability to enjoy life.

Unconditional love

It's snowing! I love snow, having grown up in the West Indies where there is no snow. It still engenders a sense of boyish excitement for me. However, I appreciate that snow creates a sense of fear and dread in many, and I want to be mindful of, and empathic with, that sense of danger. For me, I love its ability to transform – to turn the mundane into something of beauty. Yet, snow doesn't fundamentally change what's already there. Instead, it enables us to gain a changed perspective on what is already present around us.

God's love is like that too. Accepting that we are loved unconditionally – yes, *unconditionally* – by God, means that we are lovable, that we matter, and that we are of worth. This acceptance can transform how we think and feel about our sense of 'self'. It doesn't change what is already there, but it does change our perspective on what is already present within us, and on who we are. It has the ability to release the Divine potential within each of us, and to see and experience the world in a new and more meaningful way. Yet, sadly, lovc – like snow – can engender fear and dread. If 'love' (or rather a distorted understanding of love) carries with it conditionality, abuse of trust, and danger, no wonder we struggle to find the love of God easy to accept. It is difficult to trust the unconditionality of God's transforming love, because that is outside our experience of love. I feel a great sadness in this, as I experience profoundly the transforming love of God most days of my life, and so know how it has enriched my life in a very real and sincere way. But I have also known its absence in my life too, and that 'I' (or my lack of acceptance) have been the cause of its absence – not God.

Yet, each day is a new chance to work on the things that prevent us from being in a place to receive this free, unconditional, gift – yes, I do keep stressing that word 'unconditional'. Sin (i.e. the failure to reach your Divine potential) is all that's stopping you receiving that free transformational gift, and all you need to do is to forgive yourself to begin anew (i.e. to be redeemed). You are already forgiven by God. It's your own forgiveness that you need now. I make it sound so simple, but I know it isn't. It's like trying to take we not listen when it is tired, or disconnected from God, or run down? Our body, through these things, is telling us something about the state of our soul.

So, at this Easter time – a time of (re)creating – may we listen to the tacit wisdom of our body, and let go of unhealthy habits and psychological 'scripts' which hold us in a place of non-creation. In order to embrace the resurrection of our spirit, what do we need to crucify? Can we see Lent as a time of preparation in finding equilibrium for our body, as well as our soul?

Unpredictability

As I look out on the world from the frenetic TV coverage and from behind my computer, I find myself in the midst of unpredictability. The supermarket shelves are largely empty unless you live on junk food, sweets, pop and alcohol; Church worship and gatherings are prohibited in the interest of keeping the vulnerable safe; my university has closed for face-to-face teaching; I am 'sort of' self-isolating as I am in an 'at risk' grouping with my asthma, and my father is too because of his age and diabetes. So, I am working from home; pastoral visiting is by telephone; and research supervision is by Zoom. There are some advantages for me – as an academic. I have time and space to work on my next book and to write some articles for publication. Yet, it all seems so strange to my generation and those who are younger. Those who have lived through World Wars, have experienced something similar as children – only, this time, the 'enemy' is invisible, and could actually be within those we love. It is weird and unsettling, anxiety-provoking and concerning. How many will lose their jobs? How will societal life, as we have known it, recover?

... And yet, as I look out again on the world from the safety of my Sanctuary, the spring plants are coming up; the squirrels are playing; the cat is still always sleeping and snoring; the days are getting noticeably longer; the weather is getting a little warmer; and many things are very 'normal'. My sense of 'panic' dissipates a little, although I notice that the worry is still in the background. Where is my faith?

It has struck me that this enforced period of 'time for reflection' has come during Lent. As I have had to clear away much of the 'triviality' and distraction from my life, I have had to face my vulnerability; my fragility; my existential aloneness; and questions about death and dying. I have had opportunity to discern what is important in life. I have tried to do that with honesty and to face the fear – and I have found my prayer life to be immeasurably enriched because of it. Rather than fill the time with cleaning, gardening and wondering what there is to do, I have found more time for God. It hasn't been a comfortable time, but it has been an important one. It has been an opportunity to enable Lent to be what it should be – a time of honest discernment and soul-searching,

The second spiritual truth was around the vulnerability of our connection with God. Living with that day-to-day connection with the source of our being, and with our life energy, is fundamental to me in my life. Yet, how easy it is for others to put a metaphorical sledgehammer (or garden fork) through it – and threaten it. However, as people for whom faith is meaningful and precious, the importance of maintaining that connection to God is crucial – and needs nurturing and protecting.

I am glad that my cable was spared, as I am glad that my faith is still strong after the ravages of continual attack. I rejoice that I am still connected. I have adapted to the new fence, as I seem able to adapt to challenges of faith. In fact, I am now able to see benefit in my new outlook. Sometimes, what can feel like drastic challenges to faith, can enable new and valued perspectives to emerge; and my garden, and my faith, are still beautiful and precious to me.

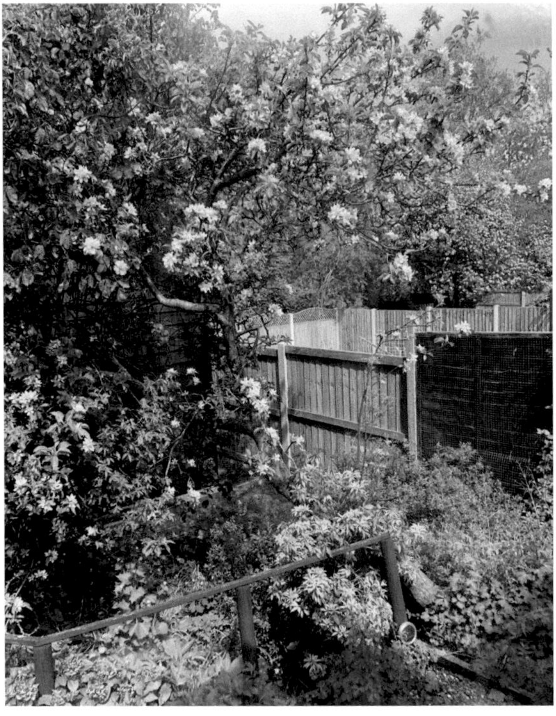

Seeing beyond the words

I am often dismissive of the book of Leviticus, because the details of it seem to have little relevance for us today as Christians. It is a book in the Bible which features little in the lectionary readings, so we don't have many sermons that are based on that book in our Sunday services. It contains mainly a series of regulations for worship and religious ceremonies from ancient Israel, and it regulates ways of living and worshipping so that people could maintain their relationship with God. It came more recently to my attention during the recent exploration of issues relating to human sexuality, because it contains some comment about same-sex relationships and other sexual practices. Perhaps the most famous words to come from Leviticus are "*Love your neighbour as you love yourself*" (19:17–18) – words that are often attributed to Jesus, and yet by uttering them, Jesus was merely quoting the early scriptures that evolved out of the formation of the establishment of Israel as a coherent community, based on a belief of what was God's Will – and therefore God's law.

For those Christians who believe that the Bible should be taken literally, there are many challenges in living out the detail in Leviticus, because ordinations should be rather bloody affairs with the killing of many animals involved. According to Leviticus, sin offerings are to be made every time we sin, and there is much about animal sacrifice and about how animals are to be eaten, which most Christians don't live by today. There are even instructions about what to do with mildew in your house, and how to purify oneself from skin diseases – and even what to do with unclean bodily discharges! Much of it is of historical interest in its detail, but of little relevance spiritually for now, if it is taken 'literally' (in my view).

However, looking more deeply at Leviticus, one can get a real sense of the deeper spiritual wisdom that lies at the heart of the book – which I believe *is* relevant for today; and that wisdom is in the beneficial nature of living with an awareness of God, and of 'holiness', which needs to be at the centre of our living. How often do we think about God in the detail of what we do *before* we do anything, or make any decision? Yet, repentance, love and renewal. I have also had to face how vulnerable my faith sometimes feels, and I have taken some comfort from the story of the Road to Emmaus, found in Luke 24:13–35, which has a theme of walking from the sunset into the sunrise – a spiritual resurrection for the two disciples.

In this event, we have these two disciples walking away, perhaps more than a bit disillusioned about the whole Jesus 'thing'. Wobbles of disillusionment and questioning as we travel *our* roads to Emmaus (so to speak), are a natural part of our human and spiritual journey as our narrative gets refocused or distorted (as it is now). One of the most puzzling, but most consistent features of the resurrection appearances of Jesus, is the fact that so many of his followers did not recognise him when he first appeared. Mary mistook him for the gardener by the tomb, and now here we have two disciples who also fail to recognise him at first. They are walking along and discussing the recent events in Jerusalem; and in the midst of their walking, Jesus himself comes along, without making a particular announcement about his arrival; and like so many of us, "*their eyes were kept from recognizing him*".

Perhaps they were absorbed in their grief and disappointment, or confusion (just as we are), over what they thought would turn out differently. They had hoped God would do 'this' or 'that'. It is such a common experience – we had hoped for this or that, but we are disappointed in our hope. It sometimes takes some refocusing from our narrative of hope to find Him, as it took the disciples some refocusing in order to see Jesus. Yet, Christ comes to us all along our journey. He is always there in the midst of the mess with us.

Maybe, what is happening around us will give us a chance as a society to refocus our priorities and address global warming; to evaluate our need to travel as much; to redress the shadow side of globalisation; and to recognise the importance of community – and maybe it is also a personal opportunity for our own reflection and renewal; to face what really matters in our lives; to grow in faith; and to reach out in love to our neighbours. Maybe our societal resurrection will be a kinder, more compassionate and less individualistic society? What will our own personal resurrection look like, I wonder?

Living Easter

It is so lovely to see the sun shining, and to feel its warm rays; to see the flowers blooming, the birds nesting, and the lambs frolicking; to hear the woodpecker tap-tap-tapping away, and to see the hedges and trees coming back to 'life' after a winter lockdown. It is fortunate for us that, in this country, Easter coincides with spring. It is easier here, than elsewhere in the world, for Easter to be a season of hope, because spring is also a season of hope – where we breathe in deeper the life-giving energies that are around us, strengthen our attitude of gratitude for what is, and foster our hope in what is to come. Our 'faith world' mirrors our external world. That is not quite the same for those who live in Australia or New Zealand, who are heading into autumn and winter. Perhaps, that is one of our many blessings of living in England!

As human beings, it is easy for us to get caught up in the victim mentality and 'woe is me' which seems rife in society around us – particularly at this time of lockdown. It can pervade our minds and our souls, so that we embody negativity without realising it. And, yes, there is much suffering in the world, and in some personal lives, of which I want to honour and be sensitively mindful. However, there is also a whole 'industry' of vested interests out there that tell us, through the media and social media, that our lives are dire, and that we need to blame someone, or hold someone to account, if things aren't quite as we expect them to be. Yes, of course, extra support is always good to have in all areas of life, but children and young people (and us) are far more resilient than we believe; if not, building resilience can be taught. Even through this pandemic, there have been many, many blessings around us. What have been your blessings? Can you identify your own?

As Christians, living with an attitude of hope, trust and love, is what identifies us as being 'different' to those of no faith. Does such an attitude identify you? Would others say of you, that you carry in your body, and in your life, an embodied attitude of hope, trust and love? Because surely that is what resurrection and Easter is about! Through strengthening our faith in Lent, and through knowing the sacrifice of Christ that we read about in Passion Week (or Holy Week), we can know that no matter what the world throws at us – and Jesus endured truly harsh suffering on Good Friday, and in the week leading up to his crucifixion – we can rise above our comparatively minor struggles, and hold on to the hope in our Saviour – who is alive, who loves us, and is with us, even in eternal life. So, let us celebrate the 'risen-ness' of our Lord – and celebrate the hope that that brings – and live with that hope in our hearts, and with an attitude of appreciation for what is. Let us live Easter!

Community

I am no 'twitcher' – but I do love watching birds. In spite of my ignorance about them, I am blessed in that where I live I am surrounded by a magnificence of birdlife. My cat has a fascination for birds, but my admiration is very different from hers! As I step out of my front door at 5.45am to go to work, I am greeted with the cacophony of the dawn chorus. It captures my attention for at least five minutes before getting in my car to face the traffic of the motorway. What composer could replicate such wonder? If I am lucky to be at home in the evening before dark, I rejoice in the sight from my conservatory of flocks of starlings dancing and pulsating as one black mass across the dusking sky. In spite of the many 'blessings' that they leave on my car, I am filled with awe and wonder by them. They truly contain the fingerprint of God. One just has to observe, and take in, the beauty that is about us. We can learn so much about God, and His intention for humankind, from such wonder. I can truly relate to the hymn writer when he says "When I in awesome wonder, consider all the works Thy hand has made ...". It is utterly inspiring.

One of the things that saddens me about our society is its lack of community. I live in a road where I know about five people by their first name, but I know nothing about them – nor do they know anything about me. That is not an uncommon experience. Yet to look at the starlings, and to hear the natural chorus of birdlife in the morning, teaches us about what wonder can be achieved when we exist in community. Our inspiration in the renewed Moravian Church, Count Nicholas von Zinzendorf, put community right at the centre of Moravian spirituality – building the settlement at Herrnhut on which our settlements in this province are modelled. However, we do not have to live in a settlement to be a community. I have been struck by our care and concern for each other in the Church, shown through simple (but nonetheless significant) acts of visiting, and through acts of reaching out. Those in Care Homes, who are no longer able to get to Church, appreciate the visits that they receive from us. One person that I recently visited, after receiving home communion said, "It's just so lovely to have something so familiar and comforting in this place! I really miss Church!" May we continue to offer our sense of community and care to each other; but may we also think about how others can be part of our community, so that we can flock and pulsate like the starlings, and sing like the dawn chorus – offering the awe and wonder of God's intentions to an otherwise isolating society. That is part of the Good News we have to offer.

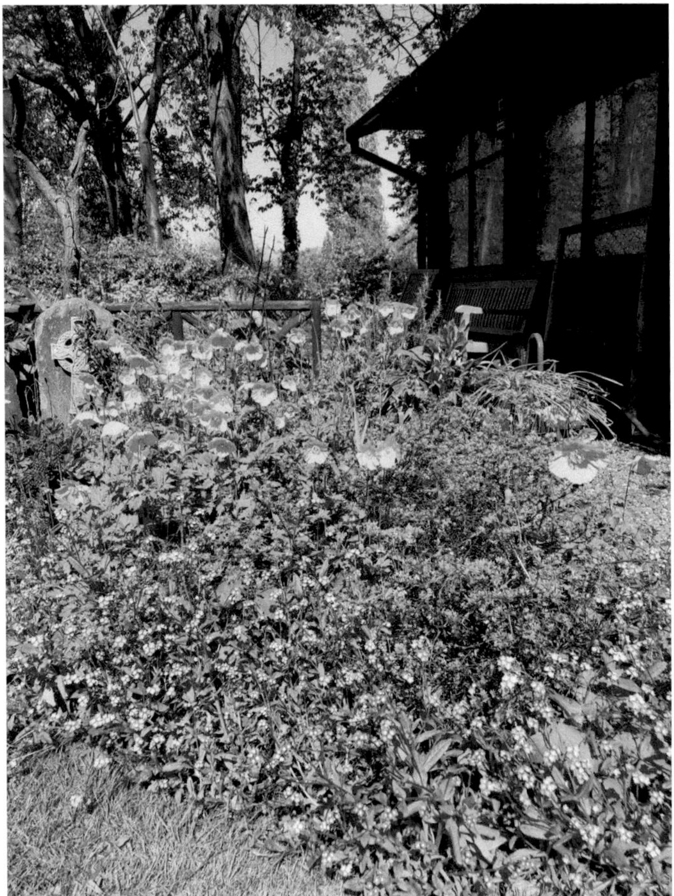

Wisdom or faith?

"Oh ye of little faith!" are words that have been said many times over the years to me by my father, from me being a boy – and yet I continue not to trust (or have faith). Why, when after so many years, I have seen the evidence for myself that things will ultimately turn out fine? They may not be exactly as I want them to be, and indeed they are often better than I thought that they would be ... yet I have planned, over-planned and catastrophised – rather than trust and have faith. I have sort of befriended this process by telling myself that if I think and plan for the worst, then it will never be as bad anyway ... So, I do (at some cost to myself)! But why is it so difficult to trust, and what is the way forward with this dilemma?

What has brought this reflection to mind, is getting ready for Easter. The ideal would be to prepare for a simple act of worship in God's Acre, reclaiming something of our Moravian tradition. Yet, for many, it would be a novel and new experience because our congregation hasn't conducted the Easter Service like that for a while – for very valid and practical reasons. It sounds simple enough, yet ... what if it rains? How many will come? For how many do I have to prepare Holy Communion? Will we have enough glasses, wine and wafers, let alone enough baps, eggs and bacon? What if the wind picks up? To something simple, is added layer upon layer of complexity, so much so, that the beauty of the simplicity (and of God) is lost in the complexity of planning. But is planning about wisdom, or about a lack of faith? Is God more present in the wisdom, or in the faith?

There is plenty written in the Bible about trust and faith. As Christians, we are to have both. Even Mother Julian of Norwich writes, "*All shall be well, and all manner of thing shall be well.*" But does trust and faith come into play when we have planned and executed the plan as best we can, then we leave it to God (or destiny)? That sense of man being God's hands ... of God helping those who help themselves? These things are seldom clear. What seems sensible is the importance of not losing the essence of God that comes through the vulnerability of trust and faith ... yet also seeing the footprint of God in the wisdom of planning.

Crossover, or not?

In Joshua 3:14–16, we read: "*It was harvest time, and the river was in flood. When the people left the camp to cross the Jordan, the priests went ahead of them, carrying the Covenant Box. As soon as the priests stepped into the river, the water stopped flowing and piled up, far upstream at Adam, the city beside Zarethan. The flow downstream to the Dead Sea was completely cut off, and the people were able to cross over near Jericho.*"

Sometimes, in life, we recognise that our path brings us to a river, where we are confronted with the choice of whether to cross over, or turn back, or journey alongside the river until we come to an easier crossing point. To cross over, there and then, means that we may be able to continue to journey beyond. However, it is not without its risks. It may not be wise to cross over because we may not be ready, or able, to swim if we lose our footing. The flow of the river may endanger our safety, or we may have a fear of the water. It may be wiser to turn back, because at least we know where we are; it is safer and familiar – but then we never move forwards beyond the river (but that may be OK). It may also be wiser to journey alongside the river for a while, to see if a further crossing point is more within our capacity to journey – but there may not be one. We may also lose sight of the path if we journey too far up, or down, the riverbank from where the path has brought us. It may be that the new path which we discover by journeying along the riverbank is better; but it may be full of nettles and brambles, and we say, "If only I had had the courage and the faith to cross over when I had had the opportunity!" If only we could know what the consequences of our actions will be before we take them. Oh, for that crystal ball.

So, how do we discern the right course of action at such times? How do we know which path is right? I guess (unhelpfully), we only know retrospectively what the right path was – and that may only be determined by taking a wrong path, or by stepping out in faith and finding ourselves on the right path. The only guarantee is what we already know, if our path stays the same; but the 'what might have been' will always remain in the unknown unless we seek out the path that is meant for us to take. What if the Israelites hadn't stepped into the river? Would they have ever reached Jericho? What part did their faith play in stepping out? Were they foolish to step out? Does the priest have to step out before Israel can follow? I don't know the answers to such questions, but may we keep our sense of God as we journey with Him to confront our rivers; and may he give us both courage and wisdom to discern His path for us.

Struggling

I have had a few 'interesting' conversations recently about 'struggling'. The conversations arose during a group session I was leading when one student said that she was leaving the course because she was finding it too challenging. She felt that she was 'growing' away from being the familiar person whom she felt herself to be (and which she liked), towards the discovery that she was becoming a person that she was struggling to like. She didn't want to be struggling with her sense of self, and so therefore wanted to retreat back to being the person that she liked herself to be. That person, I experienced as highly-defended, masked and inauthentic – but I realised that she had needed to become like that in order to survive some difficult life events, and that was now how she defined herself. Of course, she didn't see herself as others did. She was in denial.

The conversations that followed raised interesting concepts about how much does personal 'growth' have to involve struggle (i.e. facing the difficult bits of us that need our attention in order to become a better human being – or the person whom God intended us to be?), and how much was life about taking easier options? Certainly, there is a prevailing view in Western society that one should take the easy road where one can. Why waste time struggling when one can be enjoying life?! Life is too short!

I appreciate the value of this worldview to some extent. Why continue to struggle against doors that remain closed, when one can walk through those that are open to us? Why remain in relationships that are less than satisfactory, when one's growth, and finding one's self again, may come through letting-go and liberation? Why struggle against something, when the life-energy is flowing in a different direction? But then we are faced with the stark realities in history – through people like Jesus Christ, Nelson Mandela, Mother Teresa (to name only a few), where humanity is better *because* of their struggle on our behalf. Sadly, the various World Wars are also examples of when many people 'laid down their lives' for the greater good. Where would we be now if they had all taken the easy options?

One's spiritual life also seems to involve – and demand – some degree of struggle. We use metaphors like wilderness, desert and submission, to characterise difficult aspects of the spiritual journey through which we can grow. So, how can we grow as human beings if all we do is take the easy option?

May we discern when the struggle isn't worthwhile, and when it is. Taking the easy options in life isn't always best for our 'becoming' – but sometimes they just might be what God requires of us.

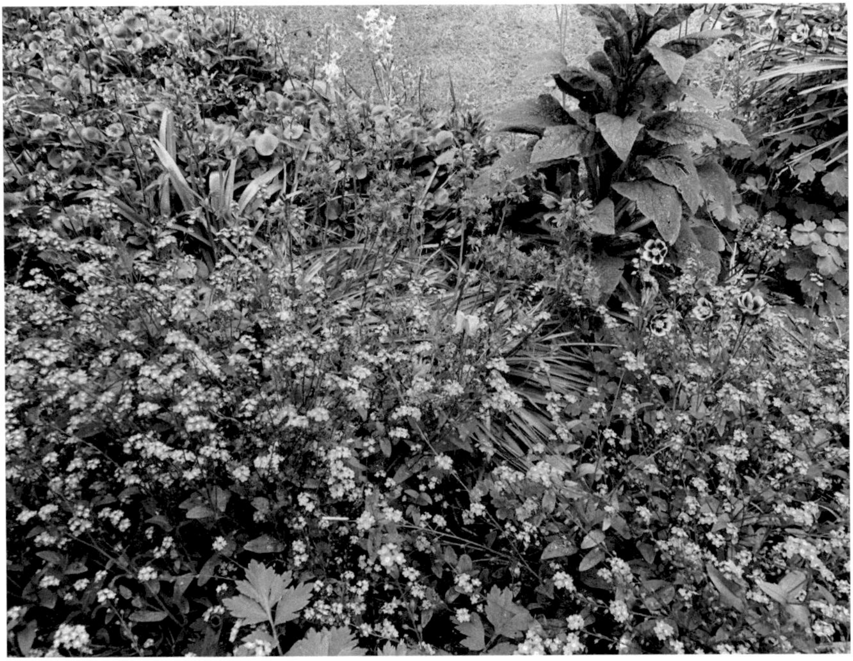

Weeds

Nature has much to teach us that is of spiritual benefit. That is why I love being in, or working in a place where I can see into, my garden (i.e. my Sanctuary). However, now that summer is approaching, as well as the glorious nature of the flowers I have encouraged and let self-seed, have also come the weeds.

My most disliked weeds are dandelions, sycamore trees (which seed aplenty in my garden beds), mare's tails, and bindweed. Yet, driving along the other day on a sunny day, the roadside was carpeted in a mass of dandelions – it was incredibly beautiful and gave me a new appreciation of dandelions; the sycamore seeds that take root in the garden beds come from a wonderful tree in the copse at the bottom of the garden, which I wouldn't be without as it is a wonderful sculpture in the winter, and offers shade in the summer; and the bindweed – well, it came with the many bluebells that were given to me by my parents from Tytherton, where they used to live – they are beautiful, and the bindweed is a small price to pay for the beauty of the bluebells. So, as I got to thinking about my weeds, I began to see them in a new, and more appreciative, light. After all, a weed is simply a wonderful plant that is growing in the wrong place (and it is only the 'wrong place' because it doesn't meet my 'wants' [or values about what should be in a garden] at the time)!

I think the same is true for any community, or group, of people – including a congregation. It is made up of people whom we value more because we like, connect with, have more in common with, or maybe we appreciate their contribution more; and it is made up of folks that we value less because we don't agree with them, we find them obstructive, or they do things differently (or less perfectly) than how we would do them or like them done. Our challenge, as a Christian congregation (and as spiritual people) is to find ways of seeing value in everyone – of finding a place in the garden for each plant, so that each can grow to its potential. Sometimes that means encouraging plants to grow where they can flourish, but can also be contained because they benefit by being contained.

Each of us has a place in God's garden. We each have our gifts and talents to bring to the garden. I can't do electrics and I am certainly rubbish at lighting bonfires with petrol, but I have found that I can flourish here and use my gifts for the benefit of the congregation in other ways. I can also help nurture other plants by making way for the sun to shine on them, or by offering shelter when needed. The same is true of all of us. We all have our gifts (talents) to offer. So how can we learn to see the value in each other, and help each other grow – including those we might think of as 'weeds'?

Grounded firm and deep

Recently, I walked into my dentist for my six-monthly check-up. I reported in at the reception and was told to go into the waiting room. As I entered, I noticed that it had recently been decorated, and as my eyes scanned the room, taking in the changes in colour, I was drawn to a new picture on the wall. It was the famous photograph of the lighthouse surrounded by waves, taken by Jean Guichard.

It was one of those moments of 'Wow'. For me, the picture encapsulated a time in my life when my world felt like it was on the edge of falling through. I had felt like the person, standing in the doorway of the lighthouse, not sure if I would make it inside to safety, or be washed over the edge and drowned. Although the context may be different, I'm sure that many of us have been to that edge and wondered if we would be swept over, lose our footing in life, and possibly drown.

Yet, throughout all of that, I had a sense of being held by something greater than me. I felt loved, closely connected with God, cared for, strangely secure and surprisingly at peace in myself – not lost in the flood of life that was going on around me. Maybe I had disassociated with the reality of what was happening, but the love of God, through others, was my constant. And when I sometimes forget and get caught up in anxiety and fear (as I sometimes do), I have this picture to remind me of the truth of God's promise – that whatever life throws at us, the essence of who we are – our spirit – will never be destroyed. God will always be present in the midst of our problems. That doesn't mean that times won't be tough, and that life as we know it may change unrecognisably, or that death may even be our path. But God's presence will be there with us, if only we can be 'grounded firm and deep in the Saviour's love'.

Hell

The topic of 'Hell' seems to have featured heavily on my radar in recent days. In my case, it comes mostly from the release of Dan Brown's latest epic, *Inferno*. As well as being an excellent read, Dan Brown's books operate on more profound levels and speak great truth – if not necessarily at a literal level. *Inferno* certainly gives much to think about – as did *The Da Vinci Code* for which Dan Brown is much famed!

There isn't much written on Hell in the Scriptures. It features comparatively few times, as opposed to 'Heaven' which is mentioned many more times. So, we can assume it didn't overly preoccupy the authors of the various books that form the Bible. It certainly didn't preoccupy Jesus. Hell isn't preached about much these days in liberal theology, and seems largely absent from modern and postmodern theological thinking. By contrast, Hell featured significantly in Victorian theology and preaching, and certainly seems to have been a significant preoccupation of the Renaissance Christian world which was emerging from the Hell of the Dark Ages. It also featured greatly at a time when the Church was most politically powerful in Western history (and where the Church is still very powerful). We can presume it was/is 'pushed' as a concept to give the Church greater political power – after all, the Church can/could 'save' souls! Hell engenders 'fear' of a place from which all souls need saving! So much so, that people even paid for forgiveness (a 'wrong' that eventually instigated the Hussite and Lutheran Reformations) and avoided conflict with the Church authorities so as not to be excommunicated – which was a certain pathway to Hell according to the thinking of the time (and in the Catholic and Evangelical Church today). Hell certainly is a powerful threat (a political tool, perhaps?), and he who holds the key to 'salvation', holds the key to much power in the minds of the unenlightened.

So, does Hell have a place in our thinking about God now? If it does, my struggle with it is to connect a belief in a God that loves unconditionally, with one who can 'condemn' us to Hell. The two cannot be reconciled in my thinking. Instead, my current view on Hell is that if a person is able to receive God's love, then they are able to live in relationship with 'Love' (God). To live in God's love is to live with an awareness of God's presence (i.e. Heaven – whether it be the Kingdom of God in the here-and-now, or the life-hereafter). A person who is unable to receive God's love (for whatever reason) although being in God's presence, will never be able to see it or experience it, until they become open to its life-enhancing possibility (that is what I understand by 'salvation' and 'redemption' – that openness to relationship with God that is, in and of itself, life-enhancing, transformational and healing). That absence of God is Hell. Hell, very simply, is to be without God – not in the sense that God is ever absent (omnipresence), but He/She/It is nonetheless *experienced* as being absent through non-awareness and absence of relationship. I experience this in clients who are unable to love themselves – no matter how much love is directed towards them and surrounds them. Their inability to 'unconditionally self-accept' means that they can't receive the love of others because they haven't yet learned and experienced that they are lovable. That means that they live in a state of not feeling loved (to them it is a state of not 'being loved'), because they can't let others into loving relationship with them. That consequential isolation and self-loathing is their Hell. This jeopardises every relationship that they have the potential to form and of which they are a part. Yet God is there (as we are there), pouring out His/Her/Its love to them *and to us*.

So, can we receive Him/Her/It as He/She/It gives His/Her/Its Love to us? How open are we to this Heaven that God offers us? That is my thinking (my 'truth') about Hell which is still evolving as my faith develops. What is your 'truth' about Hell?

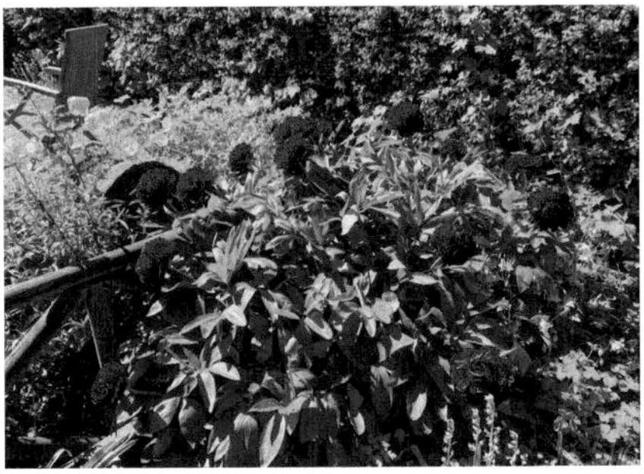

Flow and ebb

A recent trip to a tidal river, on the coast of North Wales, brings to mind the constant flow and ebb of life – the times of coming and going; of decline and regrowth. Like the sea and the river, our life does not stand still. Sometimes things are going well. We feel blessed. It is easier to have faith in these times of 'flow' (although sometimes God may feel less relevant as we are more able to stand on our own resources than trust in Him/Her/It). Then 'ebb' occurs; when life is experienced as more fragile, and we feel more vulnerable. Our sense of God can get lost in a descending fog. Life seems less sure. Sometimes, if we stand in a place on a tidal river where the outgoing fresh water competes with the force of the incoming salt water, we see how this flow and ebb creates turbulence and eddies, currents and disturbance. Which will prevail – the flow or the ebb?

Such flow and ebb are a natural part of all human life; and of the Judeo-Christian story. Studying the plight of the Israelites at the time of Moses, we see destruction and genocide, followed by rescue and then a wandering in the wilderness; then they enter the Promised Land. Throughout, God provides. This pattern of orientation, disorientation and re-orientation is played out time and time again. But what is the point and purpose of it? Where is God in it?

Looking at the effect of this flow and ebb on the many stones that line the shore, we can see a reshaping caused by this process. Some parts of the shore are transformed (especially by strong storms and tides); other parts remain firm but are tested (like the granite cliffs). The rough edges on the stones are made smooth by the to-and-fro abrasive action of flow and ebb. Seaweed is plucked up by the force of the tide, but although it causes destruction for the seaweed, it creates easy, essential and life-giving 'pickings' for wading birds and other sea creatures.

So, it seems important to trust in this life-transforming process of flow and ebb; and to learn to wait on God in the times of ebb, trusting that eventually the time of flow will come. But waiting is frustrating, and we are not required to wait passively. Prayers of lament and complaint pervade the Book of Psalms and the Book of Job in the Old Testament. We have permission to lament and complain – and to be angry with God. But if we can try and see these times of ebb and flow as 'growthful', and as a necessary process for the next stage of our journey, then that can help us to stay with the process and to adjust ourselves appropriately – and keep faith.

Anger

Many Christians believe that they become less 'Christ-like' when they are angry. Their thinking is that Christians are supposed to be tolerant, compassionate and understanding – always. So, to be less than those wonderful, peace-enhancing, attributes, which arguably signify 'the grace of God' and the 'gifts of the spirit', is to be less like Christ.

I guess that the Christ-likeness of our anger depends on the extent and 'reasonableness' of our anger, on where it is coming from within us, and on the impact of our anger on others. For, anger is a very natural emotion – just like laughing is, and loving is – yet, like anger, there is a 'shadow side' to both laughing and loving. Often, anger is a response to unfairness, injustice, hurt or betrayal. Is it more God-like to be passive in the face of these provocations? Does God expect us to be passive in the face of issues like abuse, evil and hunger – or might He expect us to be angry on His behalf about these matters? For Jesus, Himself, was sometimes angry.

Two passages in the Gospels stand out: most famously, Jesus overturning the tables of the money-changers who were violating the sacredness of the Temple, "*in anger*" (Mark 11:15–17). Less well known, is Jesus healing the man with the paralysed arm "*in anger*" (Mark 3:1–6), because the religious leaders forbid healing on the Sabbath, as it was against the laws which were designed to keep the Sabbath holy. What is interesting, is that Jesus didn't seem to get angry about poverty, slavery, or inequality in society. Arguably, He seemed to accept the inevitability of poverty, the subservient place of women in society, and the importance of being slave-like for spiritual life. And in these two passages from Mark, there is an interesting paradox where in the first passage, He is highly protective about the sacredness of His father's house, yet, in the second passage, He blatantly challenges the rules of the religious leaders which were designed to maintain the sacredness of the Sabbath! So, was Jesus being inconsistent in His use of anger, and inconsistent in the values around the sacredness of the Sabbath and the Temple?

Well, no. In both passages, Jesus is consistently using anger to demonstrate the highest form of Love. In the first case, anger is used to demonstrate that Love is greatest in the challenge of the violation of the sacred. In the second case, anger is used to demonstrate that Love is greatest in the challenge of the violation of a person in need – even if that need is on the Sabbath. He isn't saying that it is OK to violate the sacredness of the Sabbath or the Temple, but that to honour God is to honour your fellow person; and that Love takes precedence over everything in honouring the sacredness of God in the Temple and in human life.

So, anger is perfectly 'Christ-like' when given in Love – but it is an emotion which needs to be 'temper'-ed (moderated) appropriately, so that Christ's love shines through us – even in our anger.

Be your hedgehog

Once upon a time, there lived a hedgehog who felt 'called' to go on a journey to serve the rabbit world. He was well-established in the hedgehog kingdom, but the rabbits, who appeared kind and supportive initially, convinced him to join them – if he became a rabbit. The hedgehog felt flattered and affirmed, his ego suitably 'stroked'. He would go on this journey as it seemed 'right'.

So, he left everything, and did everything that the rabbits asked of him in humility, even though it meant them ignoring that he was a hedgehog, with all its gifts. He tried his best to become only a rabbit, but something just didn't feel right. So, he tried to explore his struggles with the elder rabbits. All they did was to belittle his 'hedgehogness' and try to convince him that his hedgehog gifts had no relevance to him being a rabbit, or serving the rabbit world.

Try as he might, it was difficult. 'I am a hedgehog – and a gifted, established hedgehog at that! Why should I ignore what I can bring as a hedgehog to the rabbit world, and deny who I am?' he thought. 'There are many gifts that I bring that are useful in the rabbit world.' But, the rabbits simply couldn't (or wouldn't) see it. The more he argued and bristled his prickles, the more they ridiculed and humiliated him among themselves.

At last the hedgehog stepped back from his growing sense of rage and frustration. 'Do you know? ... the hedgehog thought to himself, ... I am not generally an angry hedgehog, nor am I usually a frustrated hedgehog. Actually, being a hedgehog is great, and a real blessing to others! I can't just be a rabbit and deny my other gifts, or who I am.' So, against the climate of ridicule and disappointment expressed by the rabbit world, the hedgehog once again became who he really was, and who he felt God needed him to be – simultaneously wondering if he needed to make that journey to see what a blessing being a hedgehog really was – and why he needed to change in order to serve the rabbit world, anyway – because God can work with who we are.

Compromise

Very often, relationships and community are about 'compromise' and about humility, rather than about being 'right' and 'I told you so'. Often, we want our own way – or for things to go our way – and we get cross and upset when we don't get our own way, or things don't happen as we want them to. Then we have to find a new way of adjusting to the things that we can't change if we are not to have our lives poisoned continually with angst and upset.

A few weeks ago, my father and I had a disagreement. It concerned some robins that were beginning to build a nest in the compost recycling bin beside the house. For purely pragmatic reasons, I was keen that the robins shouldn't build their nest there because it would mean that the garden waste couldn't be emptied for a couple of months. With everything growing in the garden at this time of year, the bin is in frequent use. Having discussed it with my father, I thought that he would attend to the bin lid to prevent the robins – but he didn't. Maybe I hadn't communicated clearly enough, but then it was too late to do anything about it. Needless to say, I wasn't best pleased, and we exchanged a few cross words about the matter.

However, once I got over my initial displeasure, I had to accept the reality that my choices for using the bin were now limited. I had to find an alternative bin for the garden waste, learn to go with the flow of what I could no longer change, and await the hatching and fledging – however long that took. Instead of angst, I began to get curious about the process. Each morning, I would gingerly lift the lid and count the eggs in the nest; and each night, another little egg would appear. Then, on the seventh morning, I was confronted with mother robin sitting on her nest, which by now contained six little eggs. Interest and excitement began to grab me rather than the annoyance I had previously felt. It began to feel wonderful that these beautiful birds had chosen 'our bin' in which to lay their eggs, and my father clearly got pleasure from watching things unfold – as did the cat!

It struck me that if things had happened as I had wanted, I would have been denied the opportunity of seeing this miraculous and wonderful process unfold.

We have a process of change unfolding at our Church over these next few weeks. For some who are against the change, there is clearly angst and upset of which I am mindful. However, as we follow the spirit-led will of the majority of the congregation, my hope is that the changes will enable the work of our Church to develop and grow – but it is a risk. Nothing is certain. I want to honour and respect that this is a difficult process for some, and that we all bring our history and process to this change. But I pray that even though this is difficult, God is in this change, and my hope and prayer is that ultimately the changes will be positive for us as a congregation – and that we can be open to seeing new miracles happening in our community, just as they are happening with the robins.

Ministering

I was thinking the other day, whilst looking at a beautiful rainbow, that the word 'Minister' is a strange word. 'Minister' is a word that can mean two opposing things at the same time. It can mean both 'chief' or 'head of' (as in Government – Prime Minister), and it can mean 'servant' (one who acts in subservience to the will of another).

The other day I was working at my desk and there was a knock on my office door. It was 'Ged', the man who cleans my office at work. I stopped what I was doing, swung my chair away from my desk to face him, and we had a friendly chat. We 'encountered' each other. Ged had been an engineer for British Aerospace and had been offered early retirement – which he took. Now, he cleaned the offices, corridors and toilets of the building in which I work. I have always been struck by Ged's peace and contentment with life, and he and I talked about how 'at peace' he was with his lot. It shone through his presence and impacted on those of us around him. It certainly impacted on me – and I envied him – and I told him so, which made him smile. When he left the office, I began thinking about the fact that I couldn't do my job without Ged (or the work he does), and yet he wouldn't be employed without me (or the work I do, as I bring money into the institution from which he gets paid). We were dependent on each other, and each of us served the other. We both 'ministered' to each other, indirectly through our work, and directly through our encounter with each other.

In Matthew 20:26, we read, "*Among you, whoever wants to be great must be your servant, and whoever wants to be first must be the willing slave of all.*" Those are powerful words, and words that are sometimes difficult to see lived out in the politics of Church life. Yet, our interdependence on each other means that the terms 'great' and 'servant' (and even 'slave') are cancelled out, as the spiritual reality is that we are all of equal worth and of equal value in service of each other, and in the sight of God. That does not mean that we are all the same – but nonetheless, we are equally 'of value'. Indeed, our difference is to be celebrated. It is no accident that the rainbow is a symbol of celebrating difference, as well as a symbol of hope.

Sometimes the Church loses sight of this truth about celebrating difference, as it gets caught up in unimportant discussions about the ordination of women Bishops and practising homosexuals, the celibacy of the priesthood, the hierarchy of the threefold congregational ministry, or the authenticity of apostolic succession that is supposed to give theological credibility to Bishops. Our competence in ministry lies in recognising the value of each other and responding to that value with humility, empathy, compassion and love, by responding *from* God's love for us in our encounter with each other as God's children, seeking to value, and connect with the Divine within the other. That is what ministry is really about – and we are all Ministers. It is in living God's saving love with each other that we become competent in ministry and, along the way, we become the rainbow of hope to each other.

Bird boxes

A year ago, I bought two bird boxes from a stall at the summer fair. It took me some time to get around to mounting them on my Sanctuary, but I eventually did last winter. Then we waited with eager anticipation, in the spring, to see what would happen. At first, disappointingly, no bird was interested in either box; but then two blue tits checked out one of the boxes and returned time and time again. I thought that they would be the first residents, but for some reason the box just wasn't bijou enough for them, and they never settled. That box remained empty throughout the spring. However, a couple of great tits took up residence in the other box, and, in due course, a frenzy of feeding began to happen. Eventually, two beautiful, small birds emerged. There may have been more, but I only saw two leave the nest.

It was interesting watching the parent birds flying to and fro with full beaks, feeding the small incumbents for quite a few days – then, small heads began to appear at the doorway and eventually, after much trepidation and uncertainty, they took flight. Through the binoculars, I could see (maybe imagined?) the look of fright on their little faces before each took its first flight – but then, each, in turn, plucked up courage and were soon gone. Now, the box is empty again.

I wonder how much like those little birds the first disciples were at Pentecost? In the events that led up to Pentecost, they were still in a state of uncertainty, wondering how to move forwards and how to make sense of the events of Jesus' death and resurrection – and then something happened which filled them with confidence to go forth into the world, and proclaim the Gospel. We poetically understand it as "*they were all filled with the Holy Spirit*" (Acts 4:31).

We, like those disciples, have been in a state of recent uncertainty ourselves, and following government guidance, are discerning how to move forwards – both in our own personal lives, and in our Church life. Do we try and find safe ways of doing all that we did before (and there is nothing wrong with what we did before)? Or are there now ways of 'being' Church, and of living life, that were necessitated by 'lockdown', which we can carry forward with confidence into the 'new normal'?

Lockdown has forced many of us to think creatively about how we nourish our spiritual life when the usual means of doing so are no longer available to us. How can we use Pentecost, and follow the example of the first disciples, and the example of the little birds, to reaffirm confidence in our faith and community, to set forth – but also take some of the lessons we have recently learned into our future journey with Christ?

Open my eyes

"When Jesus was at the table with the disciples he took bread, blessed and broke it, and gave it to them. Then their eyes were opened, and they recognised him." (Luke 24:30).

This New Testament text comes from the Emmaus story in Luke's Gospel. Many of the older folks in our congregation grew up with the King James version of the Bible and may rather like the description that, "*Their eyes were holden that they should not know him.*" As a youngster, my father said that he had no idea what 'holden' meant, and assumed it was not a particularly good thing, since it prevented one from seeing things. In later years, he discovered that there have been times when his own eyes have been holden. For example, when we, as a family, arrived in this country some years ago, and were waiting to disembark from our plane, someone said, "Oh look, there's Concorde!"; so, I looked, and couldn't see it among all the other planes parked on the runway. Eventually, I discovered that it was parked right next to our own plane, and the reason why I failed to recognise it was because it was smaller than I expected it to be; smaller than the plane was that we were on. Its reputation was much bigger than the plane itself.

If we ever wonder why those two disciples did not recognise Jesus, it's because their minds were on something else. "*We had hoped that He was the one to redeem Israel.*" (Luke 24:21). But what they had hoped was no longer on the agenda. They had killed him.

It's still easy to fail to recognise Jesus, mainly because we don't expect him to be in some of the people, or in some of the circumstances, with which we are familiar. It's easy to pass by a drug addict on the other side of the street if necessary, or to avoid a certain hymn when leading worship, because I don't like the words or the tune – when, in fact, they may be an inspiration or an encouragement to someone else. If we stop and think about it for a while, we can find so many ways in which our own eyes can be holden.

Among other things, the Bible is designed to open people's eyes to new and startling truths about God – and about ourselves. May God help us to recognise what He's showing us, not just at special times, but every day.

What plan?

When I first bought my house about 30 years ago, the 'garden' was just grass – about the size of a tennis court. In the middle of it was a concrete post to support the clothes line that extended to the house. In a corner of the 'garden' was a severely cobwebbed greenhouse, with a 'Triffid' (a tall yellow Verbascum) growing out of a broken pane of glass in the roof. Two apple trees topped and tailed my rough-grass-tennis-court-size-of-a-lawn. It was hardly a 'garden'.

Over the years, it has gradually been transformed into a cottage garden in which I utterly delight, and feel blessed to have nourishing my life. It is a real sanctuary of peace and wildlife. It was never designed to any set plan. Its development started when I had two godchildren, then aged two, who came to stay shortly after I moved in. The danger of them running into the greenhouse glass with catastrophic consequences was real; and so a trellis was put up at the side of the greenhouse to stop them. A garden bed then had to be created at the base of the trellis, into which a honeysuckle, a clematis and a rose were planted and trained on to the trellis. Then bit, by bit, over time (but without a plan), the garden as it is today, 'emerged'.

I have occasionally planted gifts of plants from students and friends, some perennials and bulbs of my choice, and scattered some seeds 'to see what happens'; but the garden looks after itself in the main – and self-seeds. There isn't much lawn left now, as most of it has become garden beds and gravel paths. I have no idea from year to year, what will emerge and blossom, or where in the garden they will grow. For one year, foxgloves are in the ascendancy, only to be very sparse the next year. This year, Aquilegias (or granny's bonnets) have blessed the landscape. The snapdragons are about to show their colour along with the poppies, and then the Penstemons will show forth. It is a wonder to observe from day to day what has emerged to bless my sanctum.

And so it is the same with life. I have no plan of my life. I hate it when, at an interview, they ask the question, "Where do you see yourself as being in the next five years?" I have absolutely no idea! And yet having no plan, allows life as God intends my life to be, to emerge.

Often, we kid ourselves that we are in control of our lives – but that is a delusion; a falsity. That doesn't mean that occasionally it isn't worth the effort to plant something that I want in my garden, or in my life. But ultimately, it will be as God intends. There is a wonderful freedom and acceptance in that knowledge, providing that we can step back and observe with wonder, the life that is God-provided – rather than bear the frustration of not having things *our* way. I wonder how your life has been provided for, and if you can see the blessings in it?

Tapestry

At a recent retreat, I was reminded of the profundity of thinking about my life as a tapestry which is made up of vibrant, pastel and dark threads. The pastel colours (e.g. quiet yellows, oranges and pale greens) represent the ordinary, day-to-day aspects of life; the vibrant colours (e.g. strong reds, turquoises and purples) represent the times of enhancement, blessing and richness, such as times of passion, joy and celebration; the dark threads (e.g. the blacks, greys, browns and dark blues) represent the times of pain, suffering and angst which seem to be a necessary part of living.

All too often, we pay more attention to, celebrate and share with others, the quieter and vibrant colours (and those times in our lives – times of certainty and settlement, movement and growth); but the darker colours are also important in our tapestries, and in our lives. It is often the times of suffering and darkness that we try to avoid, shutting them out from our psyche and saying, 'I don't want to think about that!' We willingly turn away from, and keep private, those areas of shame and vulnerability, rather than shine the light of encounter on to them.

However, these dark threads are also an important part of our tapestry, offering contrast and form to an otherwise pale and featureless picture. So, let us embrace those opportunities to 'admire' and 'reflect on' the dark threads in our tapestry, and learn to embrace them with gratitude; and when we are ready, can we be brave enough and allow others to shine their lights of unconditional acceptance and love, through encounter with us, on to those threads that we have yet to accept and love within ourselves?

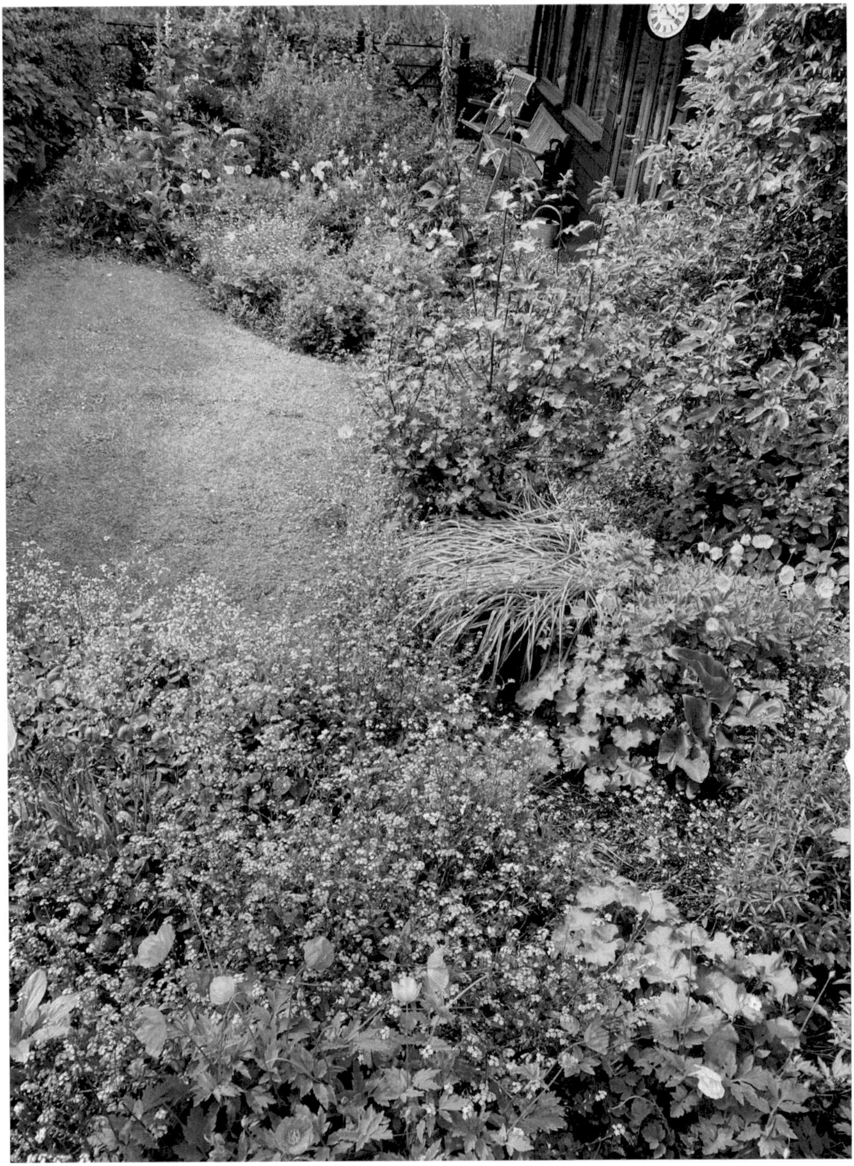

Holding death whilst living

Often, when you visit parish Churches or rural Churches, you have to enter them through the lych gate (i.e. the 'death gate'). Then you walk through the beautiful and peaceful burial (or consecrated) ground in order to enter the sanctuary and prayerful presence of the Church – the house of God.

Also, in many traditional Moravian Churches on the European continent, placed centrally between the two entry doors (one for brothers and one for sisters) is the 'dead house' (sometimes known as a 'corpse house' or 'mort house') where the coffin sits during a funeral. Traditionally, coffins are not brought into the service as they are in this country (presumably, at one time, to minimise the spread of infection); rather, they remain in a separate 'dead house' before being taken into 'God's Acre' for burial after the funeral.

Both of these 'designs' of Church (the lych gate and the dead house) contain a deliberate theology. They are a reminder that we all have to journey through death before we can enter the ultimate sanctuary of God. They also symbolically portray a theology that life and death are part of the same continuum (a juxtaposition), and we, as Christians need to journey (or live our life) in a way that doesn't deny the reality of death, but instead sees life as a preparation for death, and as a journey of hope for the life which is to come.

Death is indeed all around us, but comes more into our vision when we hear of atrocities being committed near to where we live; or may know someone who is ill with a life-threatening issue, or we may ourselves be terminally ill. Death (or its potential) brings into focus the vulnerability of life. I have sometimes felt despondent and helpless in the face of this reality, in spite of my faith.

However, I am also reminded that our faith requires of us that we hold the reality of death, and the fragility of our life, in mind – always; and that we see death, not as something to dread, but as a gateway to hope and to a wonderful life with God. I am grateful for modern science, and the miracle of medicine, that keeps those known to me with us for longer than they might have been in the past. However, I am also grateful for the reminder of the vulnerability of life through their suffering. Being alongside others in their struggle, and being in the struggle of ill-health ourselves, can help us to determine more clearly what is important in life – and the importance of our faith – and thus how we can live our lives better in the time we have left, without losing the hope which comes from our faith.

Flying through open doors

One of the real joys of summer, for me, is being able to sit in the conservatory – with the doors and windows open wide – when I get home from work. I can just sit in my favourite chair and chat with my father, with a cigar and a cup of tea (and he with his pipe) – just watching the birds and the squirrels – and the cat sprawling on the grass awaiting her opportunity to grab a passing bird. Just sitting there – watching – gives me no end of simple pleasure.

However, one of the 'down'-sides, is that the butterflies and the bumblebees fly into the conservatory, and rather than head for the wide-open doors and windows, they instead head up into the glass roof where they flap around or buzz pointlessly, for what seems like hours. I try, if I can, to guide them out with a mop (that is specially kept in the conservatory for such a purpose); but their determination to evade freedom seems so strong at times, that even I am defeated in trying to assist them out. It's as though they believe that they have to go higher in order to achieve, whilst being blind to the way that is already wide open to them. This causes me concern, because the worldwide butterfly and bee populations are under threat. I don't want my conservatory to become a graveyard for such necessary and magnificent creatures, together with everyone else's – but, regrettably, it does at times.

We human beings can be like those butterflies and bumblebees at times. We are bombarded in our education system, by the media, and by social expectation, with messages that we have to achieve and aim 'higher' – financially and inspirationally; to work hard and play hard in order to be happy and to fulfil our potential. Yet, that often causes us stress, mental health problems, inner pressure and strife – and for what purpose? So, we can have a bigger salary and a better car, or a bigger house? What value are they, if we are unhappy and worn out? Simple pleasures are looked down on. Being out and about for much of my time, I rarely go on holiday when I get annual leave, but instead I enjoy just being at home with friends when I can be. However, on return to work, I have to endure the quizzical looks that silently say,

'There must be something wrong with you!', when I am asked where I have been on holiday and I reply, "I just stayed at home."

Sometimes, like the butterflies and the bees in a conservatory, we are locked into ways that are futile and stressful, whilst being blind to the ways that are already open to us – and where God's spirit is often already. Yet, the ways that are open to us are where our life energy can often flow best – because it is where our freedom and journey ahead lies, and often where God's purpose for us lies too. That is not to say we shouldn't try to do 'something more' and achieve 'something better'; but after doing so – especially if it becomes futile and is costly – it is important to 'stop trying'. Instead, reflect on where our gifts and talents already lie, because those doors and windows are already open for us to journey forwards through. I wonder in which areas our futility lies; and what doors and windows are already open to us as individuals – and as a congregation? What are we already doing well – which is spirit-filled and God-led – that we can continue doing well or even better? I hope you enjoy your summer with a newly-found freedom – if not in body, then certainly in mind, attitude and heart; for it is important not to try to fly through a glass roof that is closed to us, but instead to find our open doors.

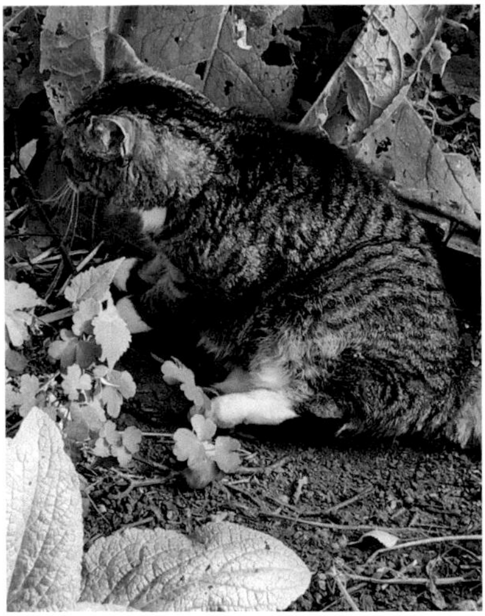

Giving sacrificially

I have been reflecting on if I give sacrificially to God – not just with my time and gifts (which I, like others, do willingly), but with my 'gold and silver'? When was the last time that I gave sacrificially to the Church? Those reflections then led me into thinking: do we, as Christians, know how to give sacrificially to God any more – or have we become too comfortable and self-centred, where our money is concerned – and we just give God the leftovers?

Church shouldn't be about money, and about fundraising – although the fellowship gained in fundraising events is often good, and the events bring some people into contact with the Church. However, when was the last time that any of us went without a holiday in order to pay for a Church project substantively? When was the last time any of us forwent the installation of a new kitchen, or conservatory, at home, in order to pay for a new kitchen facility within the Church? When was the last time that we didn't buy the new car, or the new flooring, that we were saving for, because we wanted the Church to have something lovely and useful in the service of God – without the need for fundraising?

Many of the lovely buildings in which God is worshipped, were built because people gave sacrificially – and they weren't just rich people who could afford a bit of philanthropy (although some were). Fairfield settlement was built because John Lees sold three coalmines in order to finance the building of the settlement, and others also gave sacrificially as they could. Zinzendorf spent most of his fortune to establish the Moravian Church, building settlements like Fetter Lane and Fulneck from his own money. Others also contributed generously. They did so, because they could, and out of a response of gratitude to God, for what God has done (and does) for them. They weren't concerned about "*laying up wealth on earth*" (1 Timothy 6:17–19) and making life 'comfortable', but gave all they could in gratitude for what Christ had done for them (Matthew 19:16–24). We seem to have lost sight of that sacrifice – and our response to it, through faith.

So, how much do I really believe that to be 'poor' in the things of earth, is to be 'rich' in the things of heaven (Luke 6:20)? Having grown up in the West Indies, I have seen proper poverty, and I have also met among those who are *very* poor, a strong sense of faith – and of giving generously from the little they have. So, why do we, who are relatively well off and comfortable, always look to others to pay for our Church – when God gives us so much?

Not risk free

This 'summer', so far, we have had strong winds, lightning and thunderstorms, as well as torrential rain – all of this coming on the back of some glorious weather around Easter which left me wondering if we might have been in for a drought this summer, as moors began to catch fire with the dryness! We certainly needed the rain then ... What would we do without water?

Then, being caught up in the aftermath of Covid-19, and sitting, watching the lightning, fearing it may strike the house, and fearing how the trees might be blown down in the strong winds, it highlighted just how vulnerable I am as a human being. In spite of all our precautions (e.g. masks, social distancing, lockdown), it just takes a cough or a sneeze, or a touch of a contaminated surface, to give us Covid – and then we are dependent on the state of our health and genetics to give us a good chance of fighting and surviving it.

Life is not risk free – and sometimes it is seemingly a lottery. Some years ago, I did some voluntary work in the information centre of a hospital, and having read pretty much all of the leaflets of the various diseases out of boredom, I did wonder how any of us ever remained healthy! Yet, we do survive for much of the time.

But fundamentally, we are fragile and vulnerable – we are in God's hands. When I step back from all the fear and vulnerability, I regain the psalmist's thoughts in Psalm 8:3–4, "*When I look at the sky, which you have made, at the moon and the stars, which you have set in their place – what are human beings, that you think of them; mere mortals, that you care for them*?" We are in God's hands.

So, may His hands hold us tenderly and lovingly. May He protect and guide us through this 'stormy' patch, so that we find His strength in our vulnerability.

Encounter

It never ceases to amaze me how much God is present in the everyday, and how S/He is to be found in the most unexpected places and situations – if we have eyes to see Him/Her.

A few weeks ago, I took delivery of a Kia e-Niro (an electric car to replace my diesel car – doing my bit for the stewardship of the planet, so I thought). I then made the unwise decision of doing a long journey the day after delivery. It was unwise because I hadn't yet 'learned', and adjusted to, the differences of the car. I just confidently thought I would pick them up and overcome them as I went along. Whilst the car itself was great, I hadn't realised just how poor and frustrating the infrastructure was around the country, for recharging electric cars, and, on top of that, I had two nonagenarians with me on the otherwise unplanned journey. The purpose was to take my father and my aunt, who now lives in Leicester, to see my sister in Suffolk. It was a 500-mile-round trip that would require two battery recharges; one going, and one coming back.

What I discovered (the hard way) was that not all of the charging points, that I found, worked (when we could find them!); that they were owned by different firms who each expected me to download their 'app' on to my mobile phone and give them my bank details, etc., which I refused to do; whereas, I naively thought I could just turn up, swipe my bank card at the 'pump' as in a petrol station, and recharge – not so! Also, the charging 'nozzles' are not yet standardised. So, I had to find the right 'fit' of nozzle alongside a recharging point that would take my bank card. It was like looking for a needle in a haystack! Needless to say, it was an incredibly problematic and stressful journey, and a lot of praying, and possibly 'luck' (I'm sure that God's hand was in it), got us safely home – but that wasn't guaranteed at some parts of the journey as the battery charge in the car headed uncomfortably close towards zero. I thought I'd have to be brought home, in the middle of the night, on the back of an AA truck, with two nonagenarians and me asleep in the car. Thank God that didn't happen, but it was close, and traumatic.

However, when I did find a charging point that worked – and which took my bank card, and the nozzle fitted – what I discovered was a community of people gathered around it with whom I would probably never otherwise have engaged. Because recharging took quite some time, we chatted about many topics. This provided an opportunity for us to recharge our personal metaphorical batteries too – to stop, to breathe, to have conversation, to destress, to take in the sun's rays, and to commune with God. It really struck me that misfortune and circumstance can provide opportunity to be more in tune with, and connected to, God, and to others, in encounter.

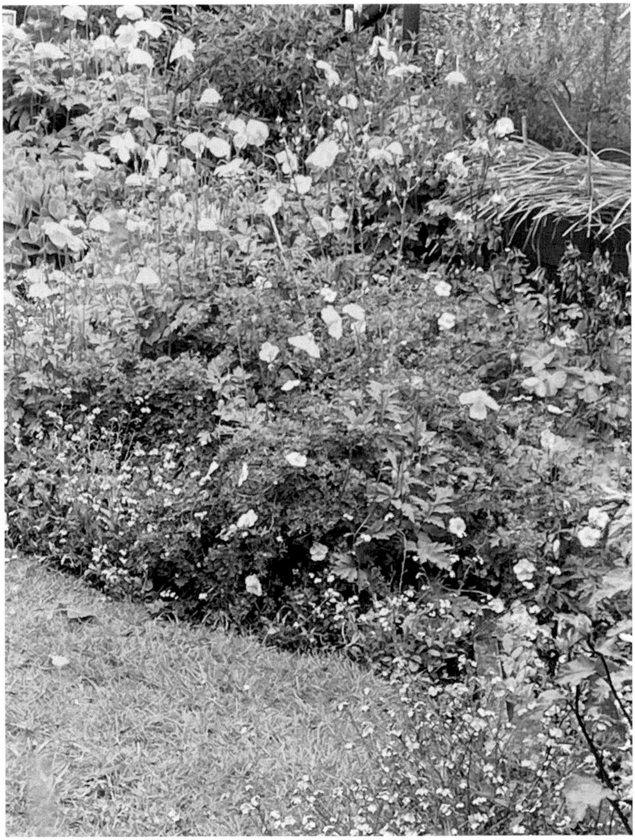

Outsider

On my two trips to Europe over the summer (Zeist and Herrnhut), I have been very aware of feeling 'the outsider'. Being unable to speak the majority language has meant a reliance on others to either attempt to speak English to the limited extent that they can, or to translate. When I have been in the midst of those who can't speak English and there is no one to translate, I have felt very alone, vulnerable and fragile. It has heightened my empathic awareness of those who are 'outsiders' in our community, whilst recognising the limitations of that empathic awareness. Although I have been unable to speak the majority language, I have at least (since we left the West Indies) been amongst the majority colour, and been blessed enough materially to cope and have a roof over my head. I have been educated enough to be able to use my wits and personal capacity to survive and earn money, and had the good health to continue in whatever life had dealt me. I have not had to struggle as some have had to; I realise that.

But being the outsider brings with it certain vulnerabilities, and a dependence on others to assist in the tasks that we can normally take for granted. There was one occasion when I felt utterly frustrated when I was saying something, but had to be put on 'pause' whilst it was translated into two languages, before I could continue. Whilst I appreciated the necessity of it in communicating with others, it interrupted the flow of the profundity of what I was trying to communicate, and I wondered why I had bothered in my frustration. During a coach trip, everyone was playing a game in which I couldn't participate. I realised how alone and cut-off I felt.

Sometimes, it can feel like that with faith. Having an idiosyncratic (i.e. individualistic and non-traditional) spirituality seems to be generally acceptable in our society. Having a belief in some faith-traditions (e.g. Buddhism) is currently in vogue; but being a Christian (or Muslim, or Jew, or Hindu, or Sikh) is sometimes considered to be suspect, potentially divisive, slightly weird, or at least toxic to the general well-being of society in some way. After all, it is sometimes said that we religious people start wars – and there is some truth in that

– but it is not the whole truth. One can feel an 'outsider' for having a Christian faith in a post-Christian Britain.

Yet, Christ was certainly an 'outsider' in his community of Orthodox Judaism, and certainly within the Roman occupied society. He challenged the boundaries of the accepted norms of his society; and so, we are called to do the same within our society (and possibly even within our faith as we respond to a heart-felt relationship with God, rather than a doctrine-driven dogmatism). We are not always called on to put 'self' first (although it is important that we sometimes do), but instead we are called to be mindful of the needs of others, to stand up against injustice, to help the poor and hungry. We are called, to be Christ in the world – and that means being called to be an 'outsider', with all its vulnerability, risk and aloneness. However, we are not called to be an outsider on our own. We have the community that is Church to be alongside us for support, and we have the loving presence of our Heavenly Father to uphold us. So, may you find the blessing that is the privilege of being an outsider, for Christ; and be more mindful of those who are outsiders in our society.

Lost sheep

Whilst on holiday in the Lake District, I had the experience of the parable of the Lost Sheep being played out on a fell, before my eyes. A gallant young shepherd, with *three* sheepdogs, skilfully rounded up about a hundred sheep in order to herd them through the gate, down the road where I was waiting patiently in my car for them to pass, and go through the gate into the next field. However much he tried – and I have never seen someone so energetic – there were 99 sheep who fulfilled his intention, but there was one (ironically, but literally) 'black' sheep, who wasn't having any of it! That black sheep charged through all four of them, several times (running at the dogs, so that the dogs didn't know what to do – as it was not what sheep usually do – and so they moved out of the way of the sheep!) to eventually find freedom on the fell by itself. It was literally a case of the shepherd leaving the 99 to go after the one that got away, but eventually the shepherd gave up through sheer exhaustion. I had to refrain from applauding his efforts!

Whether it was his pride that motivated him (for he knew he had an audience in those of us who were waiting to drive on), or the potential financial loss, or his concern for the sheep's welfare that led him to go bouncing all over the fell, sprinting up and down dale, I have no idea (probably all three). However, it brought to mind (amidst my much giggling at the scene, my sincere sympathy for the shepherd, and my utter admiration at the belligerence of the black sheep) the love and effort of *our* Great Shepherd for us, that he pursues those of us who stray (and we all stray at some time or another). However, it also brought home, quite starkly, the realisation that there are just some folks who don't want to be 'found', loved and cared for. Some see this as being trapped, smothered and restricted. However much the shepherd tried – and I give him full marks for his efforts and skill – that sheep just wanted to do its own thing; it wanted its freedom on the fell, and not to be in the field with the others.

Some people don't want God's love – or our love. That can be members of our own family, or people we encounter in daily living. That is a salutary thing to realise. It doesn't stop us from trying, and offering our love, so much so that we can feel hurt that what we have to offer them – with all its wonderful intention – is simply rejected. *We* are rejected. Yet, in many ways, those sheep (or people) have to find their own way – and we have to let them do this. The best we can hope for is that at some point, the sheep will realise what it is missing out on and return to the Great Shepherd (or to the relationship with us). There it will be met, as we are, by God's forgiving, and welcoming love – as in the parable of the Prodigal Son (or the parable of the Forgiving Father as I like to call it). And what did other bystanders make of the scene? Well, one lady laughingly said, "Humm ... you don't see that on *One Man and His Dog*, do you?"

Silly Bass

It's sometimes amazing what sitting by water can elicit in terms of reflection:

Once upon a time, there lived a Freshwater Bass, called Todd. His home was a large pond at the side of a village green. All day long, he would swim happily with his friends in the murky waters. From swimming, he built up his strength. Sometimes, people would come to the pond and throw him food. He would see their silhouette against the sky as he looked up. Because of his strength as a swimmer, on occasion, one of the challenges that his friends would dare him to perform was to swim so fast to the surface of the pond to see how high he could jump – and Todd enjoyed these challenges.

In taking part in several of these challenges, Todd noticed, on jumping, a world that was full of wide, open space, sunshine and green fields. There were buttercups in the field and ducks at rest. People were walking their dogs. It was a world that seemed very different to his own world in the pond; and it seemed so much better. More and more, Todd began to get restless and to think, 'I am tired of just swimming around in this murky pond all day. I have explored all that there is to explore here. I am growing tired of my friends who just do the same thing each day. I am ready to move on and do something different. Whenever I jump, I see such a wonderful world – a world that seems open and exciting, waiting to be explored.'

So, one day, without telling anyone, Todd took an almighty leap out of the pond and landed on the grass. At first, he felt the warmth of the sun on his scales – he felt the freedom that he had seen on his jumps. However, it wasn't long before he was struggling to breathe. Rather than feeling free, he felt trapped as he slowly suffocated. The shape of his fins meant that it took a huge effort to flap around the grass. Being outside of his pond wasn't such a wonderful place after all. So, with one almighty effort, he finally got himself to the edge of the pond and slid in, only to be greeted by his worried mother and friends who chastised him, saying, "You are such a silly Bass, Todd!"

"You're blessed when you feel you've lost what is most dear to you. Only then can you be embraced by the One most dear to you." (Matthew 5:4). Perhaps, sometimes, rather than wishing that things were different, we have to look for God's purpose in a situation; but at other times, we need to leave the familiarity of our comfort zone to discover God's presence and intention for us more profoundly.

Lopping

The end of September is the time when we traditionally celebrate Harvest. It is a time when we bring into focus our thanks and appreciation for all that God has provided in our lives and in the lives of others. However, our grateful attitude towards Harvest should really be a daily activity in our lives, as God is always giving to us. In a way, that is why grace is a vital part of mealtimes, in that it keeps our daily attitude of gratitude to God alive. How many of us say 'grace' anymore?

The only edible thing I have in my garden, apart from my herbs, is the apples. This year, I have had to make some difficult decisions about one of my apple trees (I have two in my garden). After years of having a climbing rose growing in one of them, which always looked beautiful, one half of my apple tree was struggling. In fact, it was nearly dead. Yet, the tree itself wasn't dead. I noticed last year that halfway down the trunk, a new branch had started to emerge. So, after much angst, I made the difficult decision to remove the climbing rose and cut off the struggling half of the tree to give it a chance to channel its resources into the thriving parts. Having taken my saw to a significant part of the tree, I noticed that what remained truly started to flourish. My actions made the tree look somewhat lopsided, but it seems to have been the right decision to have made as, within the year, what started out as a 6-inch budding branch has become a 4-foot new branch (not yet able or strong enough to bear apples). It should grow even more next year and give me more fruit.

It led me to think that it is sometimes like that in life too. Sometimes, we have to lop off things in our lives – perhaps things we have always done and felt were important – to make room for new things, relationships and opportunities to grow, and for us to grow spiritually. Sometimes, we hang on to things and relationships which have become 'diseased', but which we keep out of some sense of duty. However, if we are honest with ourselves, they have run their course and no longer nourish us (and sometimes they even cause us angst) – simply because we feel we 'ought' to keep them going out of a sense of duty, or because of a 'should' that we carry in our psyche. Sometimes, we hold on to things which keep us busy, but (if we are honest with ourselves) the busyness prevents us from being present to other things that really matter, e.g. being fully present to others or to God.

So, at this Harvest time, whilst we give grateful praise to God for all that He/She/It provides, can I invite you to use Harvest as a time to reflect on whether all of the things that we 'do', and all the relationships that we have, are really 'that important' to us; and if they aren't, can we afford to do some lopping in our lives to give room for something new and more vibrant to emerge? For God may be in the lopping – however painful that may be.

Eschatology

There is nothing more 'normal' and carefree than watching a flock of sparrows hopping around the lawn and in the birdbath, looking for insects and worms, and titillating themselves. It's as if whatever is going on in our world doesn't matter – and maybe they hold that wisdom which we can learn from. Apart from keeping a lookout for a sparrowhawk or cat, their world continues just the same, no matter what is going on in ours.

We, on the other hand, are surrounded by the real threat of a pandemic; by protests and unrest in different countries; by floods in some places, and famines in others; by global warming and plastic pollution. It's enough to give those who are interested in preaching eschatological theology (i.e. theology to do with the 'end of the world', with particular reference to the Book of Revelations), permission to have a field day – and many are – scaring the masses with their 'we are in the last days' utterances.

Yet, what we are experiencing now, is nothing more than a cyclical pattern of events that impacts our world from time to time. You just need to read history and geology to see that. St Paul thought that he was serving God at a time when the end of the world was nigh; we have had the Dark Ages in our past; we have come though several World Wars and several pandemics of pestilence (e.g. the Black Death and the Spanish Flu), and plenty of famines and floods which have reduced the population from time to time. It is simply nature's way of keeping our human numbers down and preventing the world from becoming too overpopulated. Yet, we are still here, and the world is still spinning – and will be for quite some time to come.

Instead of focusing on the eschatologists and growing scared and anxious, let us instead marvel at how our scientists have used their God-given talents to find a way through our current situation. Let us learn to see blessing in our new and innovative ways of adapting – whether they be technological or in building more compassionate communities. For God is surely in this current situation. Let us seek Him, and find Him, and praise Him, and live Him in our encounters with others. To Him be the glory!

Hang on to the rock face

As I have been 'out and about' this summer, I have been 'struck', in particular, by two trees ('struck' in the sense of creating awe and wonder in me) which made me stand and stare, wonder and photograph. One was a tree that was growing out of a rock face in Helsby, Cheshire; and the other was a tree that was growing out of a *very* steep embankment in Carding Mill Valley in Shropshire. What struck me, along with their beauty, was their sheer resilience. Both had defied 'the odds' to grow and 'become' mature in the most adverse of circumstances. By rights and by every law of nature, neither should exist – but they do exist, and exist well.

In my work as a Counsellor, I am often amazed by the ability of human nature to overcome adversity and trauma, and to grow in a positive way from experiences that are devastating (i.e. to become fully functioning and to live a good life with a sense of meaning and purpose). We call it 'post-traumatic growth'. Much of the research in my discipline focuses on the adverse effects of trauma, but there is a growing body of evidence that demonstrates the importance of recognising and gently encouraging post-traumatic growth through facilitating the emergence of resilience and 'purpose'.

For many people, faith/spirituality plays an important part in developing their resilience. Faith provides a narrative or conceptual framework (or set of beliefs) that supports, understands and helps us to accept the experience. The Bible is full of stories about people who have faced difficulties and have either accepted them as 'God-given' or have overcome them through faith. However, for many, trauma leads to the questioning of faith ('why has God allowed this to happen to me?'). Yet, some come through with a stronger and deeper faith having faced and survived their 'spiritual emergency', whilst others move away from their faith and are left feeling abandoned by God, and the Church, and are full of blame.

So, how resilient are you? What experiences in your life have challenged your faith? How have you grown through them? For if you can hang on to your rock face or steep embankment of difficulty, through faith, growth in meaning and purpose, and faith, can happen.

Harvest

Harvest, quite rightly, has been a celebration of God's blessings and goodness to us. It is a time, with gratitude, to take stock of that with which we have been provided; to appreciate, with awe and wonder, the beauty (and chaos) of creation – which helps us to appreciate the ability, and mystery, of the Creator more than perhaps we did before. God's fingerprint is on all of creation – even us! Just What/Who is it that can 'bring about' such magnificence – yet is able to live in intimate relationship with us, so much so that we matter, and are valued and supported (whether we realise it or not)? It is beyond expression and comprehension – yet S/He isn't. S/He is able to be 'felt', glimpsed, is tangible, and knowable – but not definable and able to be captured totally. Wow!

Harvest, too, is a time to reflect on the fact that growth in Creation is often enabled by offering the right conditions (water, sunlight, temperature, terrain). The same is true for us. If we are offered the right conditions of being loved, respected, being relationally-met and valued, we can grow towards our Divine potential – 'to become' who we are meant to be. However, as in nature, our growth is often enhanced when we add a moderate amount of manure! Too much manure kills nature, as it can do us. Often, we think of our 'mistakes' and 'regrets' as things that we wish hadn't happened ('If I could turn the clock back ...' 'If I had my time again ...'). Yet, that manure often offers immeasurable quality to our lives, once we can get, and see, beyond the destructiveness. Those damaging experiences motivate some: to help others; to offer a quality of relationship to others that was never given to them; to set up organisations that support; to offer a quality of empathy to fellow 'strugglers' – all of which enriches the lives of those that they encounter, enhances their life, and brings about a better quality of existence for humankind. It is the notion of 'the wounded healer'.

So, at this time of Harvest, may we see life through a lens of appreciation for ALL that we experience, and have experienced. May we put down our burdens of guilt and self-condemnation, and see ourselves – with awe and wonder – as part of God's creation; and see our experiences as 'interesting', as something to learn from, and as the base from which we can be Christ in the world. May we learn to see value in our 'manure', and see ourselves as having grown from it towards fulfilling our Divine potential.

Canal trip

I have just returned from a day trip on a canal boat. It was a thoroughly enjoyable day – one that was full of triumphs, joyful experiences, the occasional challenge, good food and excellent company. It took some organisation, but threatened to be cancelled at the last minute by a deep depression in the weather forecast which was prophesying strong winds, driving rain and everything that the elements could throw at us. However, having checked the boat out, and seen that there was enough room inside to protect us from the elements (should we need it), we decided to ignore the warnings and give it a go. And I'm glad we did.

The 'smoother' delights for me were the singing, the banter, the food, the countryside, the wildlife, and the cows peering over the bridge at us. The 'challenging' delights were keeping the boat on track against the wind, standing and steering in the rain, the occasional crash, the raising of the bridges (which took some effort) and the time of stuckness on the mud bank beneath the surface, when we thought we would never break free.

Yet, the trip would certainly not have been the same without the mix of smoother and more challenging times. So it is with spiritual life. Some Christians think, and preach, that faith will protect them from harm and difficulty – and then blame God if they feel that they are not protected enough. Yet, the crucifixion of Jesus demonstrates the distortion of such a view on faith, by placing suffering at the heart of faith. So, faith, rather than protect us, enables us to cope with the difficult times, and gives us a perspective on suffering that enables us to see it as something 'growthful', rather than something to be avoided. That does not mean that we put ourselves in unnecessary danger, but rather that we bring an encompassing perspective to our difficulties.

For me, on the canal trip, the challenges added 'texture' to the experience which would probably have been blander and less memorable without them. Rather than the mistakes being something to punish (either within myself or to condemn in others), they added an important dimension to the experience. And so it is with our lives; it is often our mistakes that make our life interesting – and make us more interesting to others (and to ourselves), and better people through having had our experiences. We can learn from them, and from those in others. So, the next time you are tempted to condemn yourself, or another, for a mistake or wrong decision, try and reach for the growth, and see the texture that it has added to your life – for God is surely in it if you can find Him/Her.

I am grateful for the totality of the experience of the canal trip. It wasn't foolhardy to go, but defying the forecast, in this case, added to the spirit of adventure – and I learned much about myself.

Not random chaos

When my dad came to live with me, I was keen that he didn't stop doing things that he previously enjoyed. One of these is growing vegetables – albeit his way of doing so is rather more unorthodox than mine, which can cause some disagreement at times. So, this summer, a small plot in an existing bed was duly allocated, and dug over, at the bottom of the garden. Bulbs were moved to other areas of the garden, and other plants shifted into other beds, or thrown away if they hadn't been 'successful'. The trees that overhung the garden bed were cut back to allow light and rain through, to benefit any plants that were sown. At my father's request, a copper strip was placed around the garden bed to deter slugs (even though it is utterly useless, my father doesn't like using slug pellets. He's a bit more 'organic' than I am). Spinach, radishes and red cabbage were duly planted and 'caged' to deter the cat from digging in the freshly turned soil. Each day, we have enjoyed looking to see what is happening. Now, much of the produce is ready to reap.

Over the same period of time, I have enjoyed watching documentaries on TV, detailing how much of our food is 'manufactured'. The factories are enormous (the size of several football pitches); the designs of the machines involved have been amazing; the infrastructure involved from getting the raw materials to the factories, to delivering the end products of crisps, biscuits, bread, etc. to supermarkets, is utterly mind-boggling. I have been struck by how awe-inspiring it all is. From seeing little seedlings emerge from the soil in the garden to grow into food we can eat, to looking at how our food is produced on a national or global scale – it has *all* been amazing.

It is easy to see how far removed from nature (or 'how things were meant to be') the food factory process is. However, God is certainly in the human ability to design such machines, structures and transport systems to feed the world. God is also in the small radish that is pulled up from my dad's garden. At this Harvest time, let us enable ourselves to see that God is in all that is – whether it is the tinned food, or fresh vegetables; the blossoming flowers or freshly baked bread that we bring to Harvest. I personally find it harder to believe that all of this awe-inspiring wonder happened from random chaos (which some scientists claim). For me, faith in a creative process – and therefore a Creator – makes much more sense.

Befriending the dark

Sometimes, it is difficult to sleep through the night when I have things on my mind. My habit is usually to fall straight to sleep, but then to wake up almost every night about 3am for an hour or so, with things, or clients, or pastoral situations, going round and round in my head. It used to frustrate me that it seems to be my pattern and my process; but now, I have come to befriend it and to view it as a productive time of reflection, creativity and prayer – a time with God.

It is interesting to reflect that in the Bible, God often comes to people in the dark – and in the 'night time' of living. These can be seen as those times of bereavement, uncertainty, vulnerability, conflict and fragility – when we are feeling at our lowest – times when, perhaps strangely, we also feel closest to God. The story of Jesus coming alongside the two friends who were on the way to Emmaus is one such 'night' narrative. The two friends, having witnessed the crucifixion, were returning home, dwelling on their loss and confusion, and trying to make sense of all that happened as they travelled. They thought that God would work through Jesus in a particular way, but God seemingly crushed their expectations and their hopes. However, alongside them on their journey, appears the resurrected Jesus. He isn't recognised at first, and when they arrive at the friends' house, it is night time. That is why they invite Him in to stay the night before continuing His journey. However, it was only after Jesus broke the bread that they recognised who He was.

Sometimes, inner strife and confusion plague our life. That is when we are less likely to be able to sleep, because we are searching for solutions or resolutions, by playing events over and over in our head. And when we do manage to sleep, our unconscious takes over, playing things out through our dreams. In all of that, Jesus *is* alongside us – although we may not be able to see or recognise Him until we suddenly have a moment of enlightenment (i.e. metaphorically symbolised by the breaking of the bread) – after which we can see God's hand in things.

So, do not fear the night and the darkness in life. Rather, seek to discern where and how Christ is at work – for He is surely with, and alongside, us if we can but recognise it.

Not a squirrel

In my observations on life, I have noticed that this pandemic through which we are currently living, seems to have engendered many extremes in society: some people are overly busy and feel extended and in need of a break, whilst others are bored 'out of their mind' and are looking for things with which to occupy their time; some are fearful of, and careful about, catching the virus, whilst others live their lives with little care for others and with a feeling of invincibility (it's only a bug and it won't happen to me – and I don't really care if I pass it on to others anyway).

Even the squirrels in the garden are displaying some extremes (but for reasons other than the pandemic). Some are mega-busy gathering and burying nuts for winter, whilst others have 'caughten-on' to the fact that climate change, and generous neighbours with bird tables, means that they don't have to gather nuts for winter anymore – but instead they spend more time basking in what sunshine is left before winter, or chasing other squirrels up and down the trees at the back of our house.

Sometimes, it is difficult to know just how to achieve a balance in life – a balance between being busy and being under-stretched; between being careful and not being a prisoner in our own homes; between caring enough and being over-involved; between caring enough and being under-involved. Life seems to be a constant balancing act – like living on a tightrope. Too much of anything is not healthy for our mental, physical and spiritual health. Life needs to be in balance.

Too much prayer means that we do not engage with the needs of the world through action, but too little prayer means we disconnect from a sense of God in our lives; too much busyness and distraction mean we get things done and achieve, yet often we are not present to those we love and for those who need us to be there for them.

Our body often tells us when we are out of balance – if we listen to it. So, listen to the wisdom of your body. Either take yourself 'away' from the crowds (the things that crowd in on you), as Christ did, or engage in a more 'other-centric' way if you need more stimulation. For life is about balance. We need to be balanced to walk the tightrope of life – and without balance, we fall off. We are not like the squirrels who never seem to fall off!

Of this world?

A few years ago, I attended some equality and diversity training, to update us on the implications of the Equality Act (2010). During it, I gained some interesting realisations. In short, what I discovered is that there are nine aspects to the Equality Act against which it is illegal to discriminate (e.g. race, sex, religion/beliefs, gender transition, age, maternity, etc.). What the subsequent discussion brought to light for me, is that there is, in law, a hierarchy of precedence – in which religious beliefs are at the bottom. So, for example, if a person holds a religious belief that a certain form of sexuality is wrong in the sight of God (as with some Christians and Muslims), and they discriminate against another because of their sexuality on the grounds of incompatibility with those beliefs, then the discriminator would lose the case if the issue went to court. This is despite the fact that they might feel that they are suffering discrimination because of their beliefs. We have seen examples of that in the media when bed-and-breakfast institutions, run by Christians, refuse to give gay couples a room – and lose in court.

After my initial sense of affront that religious beliefs were at the bottom of the pile (I guess we should be grateful that they are on the list at all!), I began to reflect on a growing sense of *gratitude* that they are at the bottom of legal precedence. Sometimes, I wonder if some of those 'of the world' hold more compassion than many of religion, when I see uncompassionate acts parading as religious acts. Maybe the Equality Act helps us to regain the true essence of what we are about, i.e. forces us to show love, compassion and mercy *legally*, at times when we struggle to find it in our hearts – when we are quick to decide against others, and go against others, on the grounds of faith.

Henri Nouwen, the Dutch Catholic priest, once wrote, "Often we hear the remark that we have to live *in* the world without being *of* the world." But it may be more difficult to be *in* the Church without being *of* the Church. Being *of* the Church means being so preoccupied by, and involved in, the many ecclesiastical affairs and clerical 'ins and outs', that we no longer focus on Jesus. The Church then blinds us to what we came to see, and deafens us to what we came to hear. Still, it is *in* the Church that Christ dwells, invites us to His table, and speaks to us words of eternal love. Being *in* the Church without being *of* it, is a great spiritual challenge.

The same spiritual challenge that Nouwen speaks of, is there for us as Christians who live in the world. The question for us then is, 'how can I be *in* the world, without being *of* it?', whilst recognising that there are times when being *of* the world can better reflect the love of Christ than being *of* the Church.

Remember – and don't forget

Around 11 November, people will be gathering around memorials and cenotaphs to 'remember'. Veterans will proudly parade with their medals; royalty will be saluting and bowing in humble sobriety; wreaths adorned with poppies will be laid in respectful silence. The last post will be sounded by solitary trumpeters, teetering with the final notes that end the piece prematurely in the way that war does with lives. It is a time of stocktaking. We will remember ... but why?

Some will say it is because it is our 'duty' to respect those who gave their lives for us to live free from tyranny. Remembering is the least we can do to show our individual and national gratitude for what they did on our behalf. Celebration of them, and their actions, on Remembrance Day puts their sacrifice at the focus of the nation's attention for an hour or so. We will show reverence, reflect a while, walk away somewhat more emotionally sobered, before returning to our normal lives for which, we say, they died. Would they think their sacrifice worth it if they saw how we live our lives now, I wonder? Where is the peace in the world that they fought for? The war to end all wars they said – twice ... and yet war still goes on.

Undoubtedly, those who fought alongside the fallen, or those who lost loved ones, will profoundly remember the laughter, the smells, the sounds and the stories. For them Remembrance Day is an anniversary – a reopening of the grief and a reliving of the past which is still very much in the 'now' on that one day in the year. But as the years pass, and the number of veterans and their remembering relatives decreases, what will the need to remember be about? After all, Britain was forever at war before the two World Wars, and we don't hold in our national psyche the need to remember them. And as Christians, doesn't forgetting play a part in our imperative to forgive? Aren't we in some way glorifying war by condoning remembering with parades and medals, sanctified with prayer and godly procession? How will our relationships with other nations heal if on one day in the year we keep dredging up the past, and unintentionally reminding them of the hurt they have done to us and to the world?

Remembrance Day is not about glorifying war. It is about abhorring war. Remembering – rather than forgetting – is an important part of forgiveness and of healing relationships. It is important in some types of relationships that forgiveness doesn't lead to forgetfulness – for if it does, it can enable 'damnation'. Forgetting atrocities leads to them being repeated throughout history. Remembering creates a barrier against repeating them. Remembering is therefore 'redemption'. Reminding the world and ourselves of its, and our, capacity for destruction is important. It prevents complacency, and provides us with the opportunity to avoid repeating the past. So, remember that when you wear your poppy with pride, you are enabling the support of those who are left. Remember that when you watch the marching of the veterans, they are marching out of respect for their colleagues, and also for your continued peace and liberation from the tyranny of war. Remember that when you observe the pomp and circumstance, and listen to the trumpeter, they are all enacting a desire for atrocity never to be repeated. They are remembering us too – for remembrance plays a vital part in our redemption and that of our precious world. Long may we continue to remember. It is our salvation.

Not insulated from the unexpected

Life does not always go to plan. We all know that from our own experiencing. That fact often receives our curse and damnation – and our fear and anxiety; but just maybe it could sometimes receive our gratitude – for if it were not for the interruptions to our plans, if there were no voices calling us from beyond the horizon of our 'known', if things did not fall apart from time to time, how would we know the work of mystery and grace (of God) that makes living beautiful?

Being in a place of vulnerability often heightens faith. Sometimes facing the fragility of our living causes us to lose our faith, but much of the time it heightens our need to hold on to something that is over and above our incapacity to cope. It is at such times that faith becomes both questioned, and yet strangely more profound and real. Our vulnerability enables the seeking, and the gaining, of the essence of what faith, and God, offers.

So, I wonder if our modern concern, with its emphasis on security and safety, is, at some level, fundamentally misplaced. In our efforts to prevent anything from going wrong, we may actually be confining ourselves to mediocre living – to a lesser existence where faith becomes less relevant and less real, because it largely cloaks beyond our sight the fragility and vulnerability of existence that enables faith to be more real. Yet, the fragility of life and our vulnerability are only just behind the net curtain – temporarily out of sight, yet only a feeble gust away from our awareness. In many countries where life is extremely fragile, and death and disease are literally a breath away, faith and submission to God's Will culturally prevails.

A lack of pain in our lives is often evidence that something has ceased to be alive within us. No journey worth taking can be insulated from the unexpected; indeed, I wonder if on the winds of the unknown come all that is worthy of pursuit.

Imperfect

Some years ago, I had a wooden cabin built at the bottom of my garden, which houses my study and counselling room. It is a lovely place to work in, and it is the place in which I write these reflections. I call it, the 'Sanctuary', as it is my sanctuary.

Once the workmen had erected the basic shed, it was left to me to decorate the interior to my taste, to add the preservative to the wood – and to put up the guttering. I am reasonably proficient at DIY, but I recognise that I am not quite up to 'professional' standard. So, I duly got the materials from a local DIY supplier, and set about the tasks. The decorating was OK, as was painting on the wood preservative. However, the guttering was a little trickier. For that, I had to screw in brackets to hold the gutters – but it has to have a slight angle so that the rain water is able to run away with gravity into the downpipes, and into the water butts, so that the garden can benefit from the water when we have a dry summer. Needless to say, I thought I managed a good job.

However, my efforts were not perfect as I managed to achieve a slight 'kink' in the guttering. It wasn't quite the perfect gentle slope that I had hoped to achieve. Every year since, I have looked at it and thought I ought to start again and get it right; to correct the imperfection, because in a heavy downpour the water drips at the point of the kink, rather than run off as it is supposed to.

But I have held off from correcting it. Instead, I have observed that the plants that are under the kink thrive more that many of the plants in other parts of the garden – because of the dripping of the water. I have also observed that the squirrels run down the slope of the roof, put their little paws on the edge of the gutter and drink from the water that has collected in the kink. Likewise, the birds are often scooping water up in their beaks at that point in the gutter. So, what is an imperfection, has become a veritable oasis of water for the plants and animals that live in my garden, on a dry summer's day.

And so it is with us. There is a story in Judges Ch. 7 about how Gideon used broken jars to defeat the Midianites, and in 2 Corinthians Ch. 4, Paul talks about us as being like clay pots which contain spiritual treasure. Clay pots are frail and imperfect. If Gideon's jars had been perfect, they would have hidden the light. As they were cracked, or imperfect, light could escape and shine forth. As with my gutter, God can use our imperfections to benefit His work. So, let us not punish ourselves when we fail to be perfect and don't live up to the standards of Christ all the time. That is not an excuse for complacency in our striving 'to become' in faith – but perhaps our imperfections enable others to relate to us better, or are actually endearing to others at some level. Whoever we are, and whatever our idiosyncrasies, gifts and talents, God can use us for His work – sometimes because of our imperfections.

Harmony

On 5 November (or the Saturday closest to that date), once it gets dark, father and I will partake in our annual trek to the bottom of the garden with some spiritual nourishment (and hopefully some 'growth in grace') in one hand, and some sparklers and matches in the other hand. Once seated, we will wait for the annual firework display in the local park to begin. It is always spectacular, and we get a wonderful viewing of it from our garden.

It is interesting to realise that Guy Fawkes Night is actually a celebration (or commemoration) of an historical event in 1605, when a group of Catholic nobles attempted the overthrow of the Protestant King, James I, by attempting to blow up the House of Lords when the monarch was visiting. Barrels of gunpowder were stockpiled secretly in an undercroft beneath Westminster Palace, and if it weren't for a tip-off to the authorities, England could now be a Catholic country (perhaps with anti-abortion laws and less same-sex toleration than there is now). Guy Fawkes was scapegoated and 'hung' for the offence, although many others were involved in the attempted assassination. His 'infamy' remains to this day as a community event, and as a charity fundraiser in many places.

These days, apart from enjoying the spectacle of fireworks and bonfires, we wonder what all the fuss was about, historically, between Catholics and Protestants. Indeed, our recent Retired Ministers' Retreat, which I organised and hosted, was held in a Catholic Retreat House, where Catholic Priests and Moravian Ministers intermingled peacefully in the break times. It did cross my mind, 'what would our ancestors have thought of it?'; because the Moravian Church came into being as a result of rebelling and breaking away from the Catholic Church, through the teachings of Jan Huss. Our ancestors were persecuted, and almost driven to extinction, by the Catholic Church in the Thirty Years' War (1618–1648). How things, thankfully, have changed!

Although some doctrinal and worship differences remain between our two Christian denominations, our Priests and Ministers can co-exist in harmony and mutual respect – with not a gunpowder plot in sight.

manufacture the ammunition, etc. when most of the men were away fighting.

War, like all traumatic events, turns 'normal' values and ways of operating topsy-turvy, and brings into perspective the principles we hold – which of them can be compromised and which can't. This is always required of us in general life, but in a more intense way during war. Where is God in all of this process, I wonder? Where is that still small voice, guiding and accompanying – but sometimes experienced as silent when we are willing it to tell us what the best thing is to do? How much more did our Moravian brothers and sisters experience that angst, as they discerned what to do – to compromise or to stay firm to their principles – or to find a way of achieving both (like the Vicar) for the greater good. What would you have done?

A poor Samaritan?

Why is living faith so challenging at times? It is much easier to 'just believe' and not be touched by the Gospel – as is the way with many Christians – but that isn't what Christ teaches us to do as His followers.

This summer, I was driving on my way to take a service as a guest preacher. Because I was in relatively unfamiliar territory, I felt more alert in my driving than I sometimes feel on more familiar roads. I was going down a hill, not particularly quickly (certainly less than the 30mph speed limit) and I registered that there were two people on the pavement whom I had to pass. Everything seemed normal and predictable, when suddenly the unpredictable happened. In a split-second, I suddenly became aware that the woman was now sprawled full-length in the road and I was about to run over her. Because of my hypervigilance in unfamiliar territory, I swerved and missed running over her head by no more than four inches at the most. As it was an automatic reaction, I drove past her and slowed down to stop; but as I looked for an appropriate place to pull over, I noticed in my rear-view mirror that the van behind me had seen what happened and had stopped to help. I also noticed that the person the woman was accompanied by had already helped her up, and that she was on her feet – so I drove on. I didn't stop.

I duly took my service, although I felt a little traumatised by the event, and then I drove home. In the afternoon, I sat in my conservatory enjoying a cigar and a cup of tea, when the thought came to me – 'you didn't stop ... you didn't stop'. I was taken back to the parable of the Good Samaritan, which, in reading, I had always been taught to think less of the Priests who passed by on the other side, and always thought I would stop in such a situation. So now, faced with the situation, there was I – the Priest – on my way to take a service (as the Priests in the parable were), having lived out exactly what Christ was seemingly warning against – the hypocrisy of priesthood. Suddenly the parable spoke differently to me. I could empathise with the Priests.

I could justify why I hadn't stopped – there was no place to stop other than in the road, which was dangerous to the traffic; I could see that others had come to the woman's aid; too many cooks spoil the broth (so to speak); the congregation wouldn't appreciate a visiting preacher turning up late; I couldn't offer any more than what was already being administered by others; the last thing that the woman would want is another spectator standing around her muttering platitudes in her moment of embarrassment. Such convincing justifications – and yet the thought of 'you didn't stop, and you should have stopped' just wouldn't go away. Was it more Samaritan-like (or Christ-like) to have stopped, or to have proceeded as I did and taken the service, I wonder? It still bothers me. What would you have done?

Living through fog

One of the lovely things about autumn, is seeing the mists settled in the valleys, or hugging the river, early in the morning. They blanket the landscape at low level and temporarily transform the scenery into something very beautiful, until the sun burns it off. Of course, some days, the same mist becomes fog, which thickens and clouds our vision, so much so that it is difficult to see where we are going sometimes. All I can see is the countless, distracting 'floaters' in my eyes when I am driving through the fog; but eventually the fog clears and we resume some normality of vision and direction.

And so it is with life. We may feel, at times, like we are plodding through fog, not knowing where we are going, or when we will get 'there'. Some folks have even spoken of 'brain fog' as one of the side effects of having had Covid-19. There are some days when I know exactly what they mean, as I struggle to focus or to think straight – when I have a headache and so much is coming at me that I don't know where to start with my tasks.

Now may be a time when you feel like your life is in a fog, not knowing when these strange times will end, how you will cope, and not sure of the direction of travel. It is at times like this when faith is crucial. Faith is knowing and trusting that these things are temporary – the fog will pass. Life will not always be like this, and the sun will eventually shine and burn off the mist; but whilst in the fog, faith is in knowing that we are held secure by One who loves us, and that we can trust in our capacity to cope.

Patient anticipation

Advent is a season that is characterised by expectation. We anticipate the coming of Christ – the personification of God in the world. That expectation is symbolised profoundly in the nativity, where all await. Mary, Joseph, the Shepherds and the Wise Men – all wait for what is to come; all living out their faith in expectation, in very different, but profound ways.

There are many times when we seem to be at an advent in our lives – not just around Christmas. Times when we are waiting, and wondering, and seeking to know where God is in what is around us. How will this situation that I am faced with challenge, confirm or strengthen my faith? What is God requiring of me now? Where is God in this?

Often the answer to these questions eludes us. Sometimes the answer is enfolded within a process of patient unfolding – yet having patience is hard. It is easier to get in touch with the frustration and angst, to act out of anger and blame. It is more difficult to trust the revelation of what is to come in God's time.

Henri Nouwen states that waiting patiently is not the same as waiting passively. It is an active process in which we live the present moment to the full in order to find there the signs of the One who is to come. He states that the word 'patience' comes from the Latin verb 'patior' which means 'to suffer'. Waiting patiently is suffering through the present moment, tasting it to the full, and letting the seeds that are sown in the ground on which we stand grow into strong plants. Waiting patiently always means paying attention to what is happening right before our eyes and seeing there the first rays of God's glorious coming.

May you acknowledge, with patient anticipation, that which is to come; and find God's presence in what is – rather than in what you hoped would be.

Reservoir

For most of us, Christmas has become predominantly nothing more than a hectic round of materialistic indulgence – even when we have a Christian faith. It saddens me to see what Christmas has become, and I find myself wanting to retreat more and more from its distortions, in order to quietly regain the profundity and essence of what it means for God to come in as 'light', and as 'infant', amidst the darkness of humanity.

Amidst the increased pressures, it seems particularly important to rediscover the peace of Christmas – to know yourself held and loved in the heart of God. This is the source and the secret of peace; a deep and untouchable certainty which is harboured in the depths of our souls. It exists there as a great reservoir which can be tapped and drawn upon at any time and in any circumstances. Once we know where it is, and how to reach it, peace is *always* available to us. By slowly breathing our way into it, descending into the depths, we can soak ourselves in the vast springs of serenity. In the midst of our seeming chaos or confusion, we are always only a few breaths away from accessing an inexhaustible peace. When we return to the surface, we carry the tranquillity with us, bringing it as a free gift to those who surround us. It is not our own peace, but the peace of God, freely given.

Dark times

We seem to live in dark and threatening times. The threat grows ever closer. It didn't seem so bad when the bombs were happening in distant parts of the world. We could get on with our daily lives, because they were 'over there'. At dark times like these, it is easy to focus in on the vulnerability of our humanity, and feel down and helpless, fragile and fearful. We open our curtains on to the world through our iPads, iPods, laptops, televisions and radios – and all we experience is that darkness in a never-ending cycle of depressing news and conversation about the threat. It is furthermore confusing, because that darkness is dressed up in the cloak of belief and religion – things that are supposed to be influences for good in the world; and our reactions are to want to oppose everyone of that 'supposed' faith, and the world seemingly wants to oppose all of us 'of faith'. "Why have a faith if all it does is bring about such destruction?" some people say. The darkness plays into our very fears of suspicion around 'difference', and the desire to turn our society into 'folk like us' is strengthened in our collective psyche.

Standing, as we are, in our dark times, it is salutary to recognise that Jesus was born into such a world, where threat and oppression reigned. It was a world, like ours, where many folks seemed to prefer evil and darkness. Into that world, came God's 'light' – the light of enlightenment. It is a light that still flickers in many, and which still shines brightly in others. Through His teaching and life, people came to know what it meant to live as members of God's family, and to know that they are related to all of God's creation. Jesus gave us a new understanding of what it meant to be alive – a gift available to *all* through grace. It shines in us when we give and don't take; when we live by faith and not fear; when we seek reconciliation and not conflict; when we serve and do not dominate. That light springs up from our innermost being like a fountain of living water. It intoxicates us so that life turns from disappointment into a banquet. This light of aliveness and love opens us up to rethink everything – to become children again and rediscover the world with fresh, childlike wonder, seeing the world in a new light.

So, let us move away from the darkness of our world, and light a candle for the Christ child – the Word made flesh. Let our hearts glow with that light that was in Him, so that we become candles through which His light still shines. Christmas is a 'process' as well as an event. Our hearts can once again become the little town, the stable, the manger ... the place where He is born again – even now. Let a new day begin in us, a new creation, a new you, and a new me. Let there be light!

Courageous optimism

My cat, Effie, is a shining example of hope. She lives her life constantly in hope. Her hope always is that whoever is heading into the kitchen will put something in her plate, so that she can indulge her greed.

Like Effie, children hope at this time of year that they will get what they want for Christmas, and employ every verbal and non-verbal tactic to ensure it. But, that kind of hope lacks a sense of certainty. It is more like a wish – something that we want to happen but have no way of knowing that it ultimately will. So, we keep our fingers crossed and 'hope' that everything will go the way we want it to. However, the reality is that often life doesn't turn out the way we hoped it would. Hope is a fragile commodity. When life is disappointing, our optimism is replaced by feelings of discouragement and hopelessness and, before long, we run the risk of becoming cynics who believe that there is nothing in which we can confidently hope.

Ironically (because nothing is new), this was the landscape of life when Jesus entered the world. The prevailing mood of Israel was anything *but* hope. The once proud nation was then a puppet state of the Roman Empire. Centuries before, they had been promised a deliverer who would restore Israel to its former glory, but it had never happened. Into this sense of cynical hopelessness, true Hope was born. But the tragedy of that first Christmas was that very few realised the hope that had been introduced. Hope for the forgiveness of sins; hope for a bright future; hope for God's presence and power in daily living; hope that would enable us to forget the past and set our sights on stuff that doesn't disappoint; a hope that, because of Jesus, is a certainty and not just another wish to be dashed on the rocks of reality.

I love the honesty of the psalmist who said, "*Why are you downcast, O my soul? Why so disturbed within me ...? Put your hope in God, for I will yet praise Him, my Saviour and my God*" (Psalm 42:5). This Christmas, let us rejoice that our faith gives us something better than the disappointments of life on Planet Earth. And when by faith we embrace Him, and all that He promised, let us have a hope that is no longer a fingers-crossed wish that we harbour in our heart, but rather a confident, courageous optimism that is rooted in the certainty of His Word.

Reaching out to be rejected again

My cat often gets teased by the birds, and it's cruelly lovely to watch. Sometimes they are sitting on the lawn when she is under a bush in the garden. They hop about seemingly innocently, whilst she positions herself carefully to pounce – and then, at the last moment, they fly away leaving her dejected and disappointed (and me feeling relieved). Sometimes, inside of the conservatory, she sits poised and watching the small birds dancing on the ledge on the other side of the frosted glass – literally two inches away from her. They seem unable to see her, but she can clearly see them through the glass, and is 'chattering' expectantly (i.e. making those strange noises that cats do when they see birds in close proximity), in the hope that they will come hopping into her mouth. Yet, the glass is between them. So near, yet so far!

What isn't funny in life, though, are those times when something is seemingly within reach, yet is so far away. Those times: like when we try to help those we love, and all they do is get angry with us; like when we see the potential in others, and they turn down what we offer by way of help, hope and encouragement; like when we see the inner beauty in others, and all they can see is the ugliness of their shame and self-loathing. They are so near (physically), and yet in many ways so far away from us (psychologically and spiritually). How helpless we feel ...

I sometimes wonder if that is how God frequently feels? That God sees our potential, both as individuals and as a human race, and feels powerless to help us when we can't see it for ourselves; and disappointed when we instead choose paths to self-destruction or stuckness. Maybe that is what Christmas is about – God offering us another way, exemplified through His son, Jesus Christ, other than our innate ways of self-destruction and self-abasement. That having gone so astray from our potential to be like God, He had to remind us again of who He was, by becoming human (incarnation) and living among us to demonstrate how transformed life could be if only we could live again by faith and love. Yet, His love was rejected on the cross, and still we reject Him. So near, and yet so far.

We know the way to truth and life. It has been revealed to us. I have that sense that God is waiting for us to *truly* embrace Him. Maybe this Christmas will be a challenge of how much importance we really give to spiritual matters, or whether we will again be distracted by the busyness and materialism of Christmas? Will we fail Him, and reject Him, yet again, by merely paying Him lip service through the tinsel and wrapping paper?

I already sense His sadness ...

My soul doth magnify the Lord

"*My soul doth magnify the Lord, and my spirit hath rejoiced in God, my Saviour* ..." (Luke 1:46–47). These are the words of what has come to be known as the 'Magnificat' – spoken or sung by Mary in response to the wondrous events that she had experienced which led to the birth of her son, Jesus. "My soul doth magnify the Lord, and my spirit hath rejoiced in God, my Saviour ..."

It is a response to a moment of utter spiritual awe and wonder. How often do we have those moments of utter awe and wonder in response to our faith, I wonder? How often does our soul magnify the Lord, and rejoice in God our Saviour? So often, we come to Church, sit through a service, and leave with what we brought with us – our criticisms, our gloominess, our anxieties and our concerns. Our soul fails to be 'touched' and our concerns fail to be transcended by our encounter with God, as Mary's was, and we blame the service, or the Minister, rather than look within ourselves at what is getting in the way for us.

Similarly, so often we enter the Christmas period carrying the anxieties of the season – our concerns about debt, about buying appropriate presents and getting in the right food – that we fail to be moved by the enormity of what we are about to celebrate – God becoming human, like us, and living among us, being revealed through the person of Jesus Christ. Instead, we turn the season of Advent – and even Christmas itself – into a children's festival, devoid of its enormous theological and incarnational significance.

So, what needs to shift within us so that we can enter Advent and Christmas, more able to experience and encounter God within our celebrations and within our encounters with each other, so that we can echo, with sincerity, the words of Mary: "*My soul doth magnify the Lord, and my spirit hath rejoiced in God, my Saviour* ..." (Luke 1:46–47)? For only then, will we *truly* be ready to embrace Christmas.

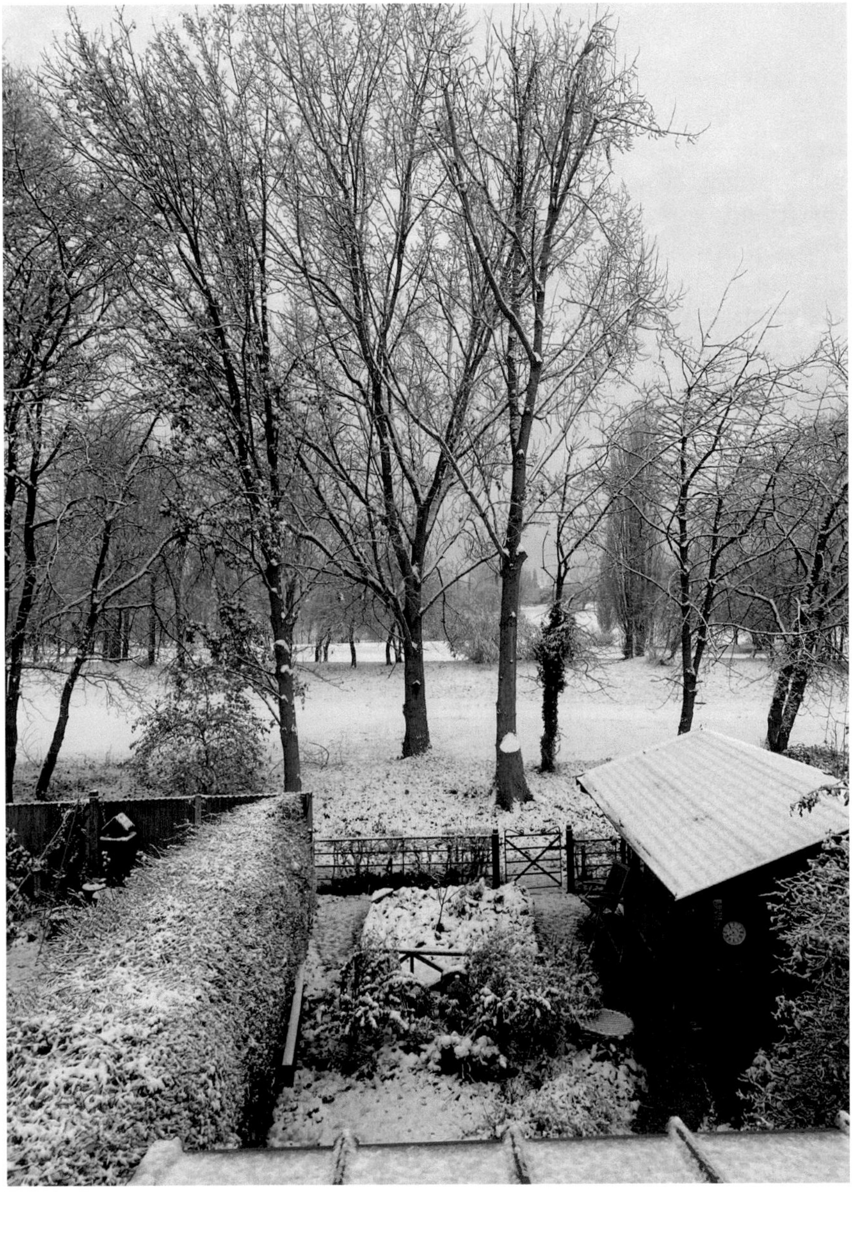

Blind to the obvious

The other day, I met a friend at Lytham St Annes, and we spent much of our time there walking along the sea/river front, embracing the fresh air, the sunshine and each other's company. At some point on our journey, we sat on one of the benches for a break. I'm not sure why my friend chose that particular bench because, to me, it had a bush growing up right in front of it which blocked the immediate view in front of us. However, the peripheral views were lovely, so we sat down and chatted away – and I said nothing about the bush.

As we got up to walk some more, my friend said, "Oh, wasn't the view lovely from where we sat!?"

... to which I replied, "Yes, it was great – apart from the bush!"

"What bush?", she said, "I didn't see any bush."

"How could you have missed it?" I retorted. "It was growing right in front of us, blocking the immediate view. You had to look around it to see anything."

"Oh ... I didn't notice any bush," she said.

We laughed. To me, it was a case of 'how could she not notice?' It was *that(!)* obvious; but for her, it was a case of, 'why didn't you say something? I genuinely didn't notice it', as she was probably more absorbed in the conversation than perhaps I was. To me, it was just *so obvious* that I shouldn't need to say anything. Instead, I quietly wondered why she had chosen that bench from all the benches on which we could have sat.

It's just one of those very human interactions that we often engage in within our different contexts, from time to time. But sometimes, something that, to us, is 'obvious', isn't obvious to others at all – and needs to be consciously pointed out. We can't assume that others can always see the same.

I wonder if Christmas is a bit like that for Christians? We know how important Christmas is to us, because we have a faith. We can see and value the theological truth of the incarnation – that God became human and dwelt among us, revealing something of Himself so that we might know Him better, know how to achieve our potential as spiritual 'beings', and be able to live in relationship with Him who is eternal and everlasting and yet who is the true essence of us. But for those who have no faith, its importance and significance often get overlooked. Christmas thus becomes trivialised and commercialised with eating and gifts, with reindeer and Santas – and we wonder why people can't see what it is truly about.

So, this Christmas, may we not presume that others know what Christmas is really about – and may we thus share something of the love we have for our faith with them, for we cannot assume that others can see it for themselves.

Mind how you tread

Mind how you tread! With so many autumn leaves on the ground still waiting to be swept up, one has to tread carefully on the pavements in order to avoid slipping on wet leaves. I think 'mind how you tread' is also a wise mantra to live by as we head towards Christmas. Christmas comes at the time of year when the year is dying – and at a time when many significant folks in our congregation and community are dying. That is not morbid, but merely an acknowledgement that what for many is a joyful occasion, is also contaminated with paradox and death. Indeed, the celebration of Christmas is there to bring light into that darkness. That itself, is a paradox.

This sense of paradox and death are very much reflected in the Christmas stories. In spite of our attempts to dress them up with cute children and animals, the narratives are full of death and paradox. We see contrasts between those who come to Christ, in the form of Wise Men and Shepherds; in the lovingness of God for humanity as against the destruction of humanity by Herod; in the security-of-self embodied by Mary that enabled her to step out so hugely in faith, as opposed to the culling of vulnerable children to protect the security of he who was so insecure in his kingdom; we see death versus life. With the Birth Narratives placing so much emphasis on the 'coming of Christ' as a baby, it is easy to ignore or overlook the death, transition, journeying and fear that are imbedded in the experience of Christ's birth.

Strange as it may seem, that gives me comfort; for whilst others celebrate, I have permission to both celebrate and grieve. The Birth Narratives show us that life is very much about holding, and living with, the tension between its paradoxes. Life and death are both parts of the same entity. That is our reality. So, whilst we rightly focus on the celebrations that make Christmas joyful and meaningful, don't ignore the fact that some are in pain at this time of year. Our challenge is to hold both in creative tension sensitively, by not pretending that the other doesn't exist; and to find the presence of God in both – and to tread carefully in our encounters with others.

Stay or leave?

"How much should I put up with bullying and criticism before I walk away?" This was a question that I was recently exploring with a pastoral supervisee. My supervisee was a priest of considerable experience, integrity and ability, but who was feeling emotionally and spiritually worn down by some toxic folks in his congregation, for whom he couldn't do anything right. As I facilitated the supervision session, I was struck by how being a Christian sometimes keeps us in unhealthy situations through an unhealthy sense of vocation and Christian 'rightness'.

I have been blessed that, in my ministry, such people have been relatively few and far between. However, when they have existed, they have tended to tarnish and demoralise the life of the Minister, and often the life of the congregation. It is like having a group of 20 students defined by the one difficult student who takes up all of the emotional energy and reflection time. Yet, it is important to not lose sight of the fact that it is only one person who is challenging, and not the whole group – which is a difficult perspective to maintain when one is 'in' the situation.

Whilst it is sometimes beneficial for the greater good to 'tough out' a situation, self-respect and the valuing-of-one's-self must also be a consideration. When should vocation and a 'sense of the greater good' override self-respect, and when should self-respect override the 'wrongness' and degradation of bullying and toxicity? These are difficult questions to discern, and the same is true of any relationship. When is it 'right' to endure an unhealthy marriage, and when is it better to let it go?

In my experience, Christians have a tendency to think that walking away from anyone, or letting anyone walk away from them, is a failure. Yet, in Matthew 10:14, Jesus encourages us to wipe the dust from our feet of those who "*will not receive you, or hear your words*". Jesus, himself, walked away from toxic people, and let them walk away from Him. For, we cannot fix every broken person that we encounter, and sometimes walking away is the only way to defend the good work that God is calling us to do. Indeed, in Gary Thomas's book, *When to Walk*

Away: Finding Freedom From Toxic People, Thomas lists 41 occasions when Jesus walked away, and let others walk away from Him.

So, may we discern when to stay and when to leave; and may we treat ourselves with the same compassion that we would like to give to everyone, but can't realistically. For although our faith requires us to transcend the limitations of our humanity, wisdom is in knowing when it is no longer God's Will for us to continue to be poisoned by another's toxicity.

About the author

Peter Madsen Gubi is Professor of Counselling and Spiritual Accompaniment at the University of Chester, UK, and Honorary Professor of Practical Theology at Teofilo Kisanji University, Tanzania.

Peter was born in Barbados in the West Indies, and moved to England with his family at the age of 12. After finishing school, he trained to be a Religious Studies teacher at the University of Chichester and then spent seven years as a teacher of Religious Studies. Discovering a gift for pastoral care, Peter furthered his studies in Counselling at the University of Nottingham, and then spent over 30 years working as a psychological Counsellor in various medical settings, the third sector, education and in private practice.

Peter eventually became an academic and a practitioner-researcher, and gained his Doctor of Philosophy degree (Ph.D.) in Counselling Studies from the University of Manchester. From being a Principal Lecturer in Counselling and Psychotherapy at the University of Central Lancashire, Peter has been at the forefront of writing and research on the spiritual dimension of mental health, and the ethical integration of faith resources in counselling and the helping professions, for which he has gained an international reputation. Peter is also a qualified Spiritual Director.

Moving to, and recognised by, the University of Chester with a personal Chair as a Professor of Counselling, Peter undertook a Doctor of Theology (Th.D.) degree in Theology and Practice at the University of Winchester and then a Doctor of Ministry (D.Min.) degree in Ecclesiastical Pastoral Care at the University of Chester. Peter has been at the forefront of supporting clergy well-being through researching and advocating for Reflective Practice Groups and Pastoral Supervision as forms of well-being support for all clergy across all denominations, for which he has gained a national reputation.

Peter serves as a Trustee of the Association for Pastoral Supervision and Education (APSE), and is Chair of the Training, Research and Publication Sub-Group of APSE. He is also an APSE Senior Accredited Pastoral Supervisor and has an established practice in pastoral supervision. Peter has authored eight books and published many peer-reviewed research articles. Peter is also a Presbyter in the Moravian Church (British Province) and has served congregations in the Yorkshire and Lancashire Districts as a Minister, as well as serving on the Provincial Elders' Conference (2021–2022), as Chair of the Provincial Church Service Committee, as Co-ordinator of Pastoral Supervision in the Moravian Church (British Province), and as Co-ordinator of Worship Leader training in the British Province.

When not accompanying and serving others, and finding God in his encounters, Peter enjoys the simple, relational pleasures of being with friends and family, playing table tennis, cycling, gardening and just reflecting by sitting, or walking, with an awareness of God's presence. In essence, Peter is a spiritual pilgrim who uses his gifts to enable the well-being and development of others.

It is amazing how faith has the capacity to heal rifts and differences (as well as to cause them, sadly, at times). May we live our faith in such a way that love, peace and harmony can reign within, and between, us – even when there is difference.

Principled

Compromise is a most difficult thing to achieve when we are principled. We see it in what we are told about the current 'Brexit' talks, with each side having their 'red lines' beyond which each side is not prepared to compromise – and there is something admirable (and also frustrating) about having 'principles'. We are taught that Christians should be principled people – but what would the world, and our relationships, look like if we all held a principled position in every disagreement and situation? Isn't compromise often better?

This November marks the centenary of the end of what we now call the 'First World War' (1914–1918). Some of the men of this congregation died in that war, and we have a memorial to remember them by on the wall in our worship space. I suspect that many of the women of the congregation endured great suffering too, but alas we don't have a memorial for them. If I hadn't been so short-staffed at work, I would have liked to have researched more about each of the lives (names) on the memorial – but like most things in life, that has had to be a compromise between what needs to be done to 'survive', and what is realistically doable in the circumstances, if I am not to go under with stress. Yet more compromise!

I do sometimes look at that memorial and wonder what each person looked like; what their jobs and family lives were like; whether any of them were pacifists or conscientious objectors (which many Moravians were) who succumbed to the pressures of joining the war? Did any of them compromise their principles for the 'greater good'? What would I have done if it were me in that situation? I was also reminded recently of a Vicar, from the Lake District, who went to the Front – not as a fighter but who served as a medic, thereby keeping his principles of non-violence – helping soldiers from either side in need. He risked life and limb, becoming the most decorated non-fighter, gaining the Victoria Cross and other medals for bravery. What would have happened to those whom he rescued if his principles of non-violence had kept him out of the war? Yet, men and women were needed to grow the crops,